A PIECE OF MY HEART

A play in two acts

by Shirley Lauro

**Suggested by the book
by Keith Walker**

SAMUEL FRENCH, INC.

45 WEST 25TH STREET   NEW YORK 10010
7623 SUNSET BOULEVARD   HOLLYWOOD 90046
LONDON   TORONTO

ISBN 0 573 69333 1   Printed in U.S.A.   # 17971

To my beloved daughter, Andrea

IMPORTANT BILLING AND CREDIT REQUIREMENTS

All producers of A PIECE OF MY HEART *must* give credit to the Author of the Play in all programs distributed in connection with performances of the Play and in all instances in which the title of the Play appears for purposes of advertising, publicizing or otherwise exploiting the Play and/or a production. The name of the Author *must* also appear on a separate line, on which no other name appears, immediately following the title, and *must* appear in size of type not less than fifty percent the size of the title type in similar fashion:

A Piece of My Heart
by
Shirley Lauro
Suggested by the book by Keith Walker (50% size of Author's billing)

The following credits must also be included in all programs distributed in connection with performances of the Play and in all instances in which the title of the Play appears for purposes of advertising, publicizing or otherwise exploiting the Play and/or a production:

"Originally produced in New York City by the Manhattan Theatre Club.
Professionally produced in the 1991 Humana Festival of New American Plays at Actors Theatre of Louisville.
Originally produced by the Philadelphia Festival for New Plays."

A Piece of My Heart was originally produced by the Philadelphia Festival Theatre for New Plays.

It was professionally produced in the 1991 Humana Festival of New American Plays at Actors Theatre of Louisville.

A Piece of My Heart premiered in New York City on October 15, 1991 at the Union Square Theatre. It was produced by the Manhattan Theatre Club with special arrangement with Roger L.Stevens and directed by Allen R. Belknap. The cast was:

MARTHA ....Annete Helde
MARYJO ....Cynthia Carle
SISSY..................................Corliss Preston
WHITNEY ....Sharon Schlarth
LEEANN ....Kim Miyori
STEELE .... Novella Nelson
All the American Men ....Tom Stechschulte

Sets by: James Fenhagen
Costumes by: Mimi Maxmen
Lighting by: Richard Winkler
Sound by: John Kilgore
Production Stage Manager: Richard Hester

AUTHOR'S SUGGESTIONS

STYLE:

The play is a style piece. It is presentational. All design elements therefore conform to this. Abstracted, suggestive, part for the whole. Nothing in text should be illustrated or literally rendered from the design standpoint.

The characters in the play are in a direct relationship with the audience. They have a great, urgent need to tell their stories to the audience and it is from this urgency that they pull the other characters into helping them tell what has happened to them. Their memories are so vivid as they start to relate experiences that the past comes alive for all of them. It is from this urgent need to communicate that the style of the play evolves.

SET:

The play adapts to many production concepts. It can be staged very simply with benches and black drapes as backdrop. It can be staged in the round with an environmental approach—the audience becoming a part of the environment. It can be staged in a more formal manner with lighting, sound, platforms and scrims denoting changes of place and time. Therefore, directors and designers are encouraged to use imagination in tandem with budgets and facilities to create an appropriate design.

In a more formal design, three platforms of different heights are suggested, plus a downstage center ground level playing area (see sketch). The use of four portable, *lightweight* bamboo benches is suggested which can serve for various seating needs—airplane seating, bar stools, chairs, hospital beds, stretchers, etc. These can be moved from level to level and area to area during the action by actors. There should be steps between the platforms, and possibly one ramp. Back scrims can be used plain or with projections—a red cross for hospital, impressionistic flashes of tracers, etc. Realistic projections, however, should not be used. Depending on the directoral concept, the play can sustain quite sophisticated light and sound cues, as well as pyro explosions. A bright red scrim is suggested for the end of the Tet scene.

If full platforms are used, it is suggested that projections on the facings of the platforms be used for the names on The Wall at the end of play. Light boxes with scrim are suggested. See special note on The Wall at end of the play text. If full platforms cannot be built, scaffolding is suggested as an alternative platform construction. If scaffolding is used, or if the play is done without platforms, it is suggested that The Wall simply be imagined by the actors as being in front of them, never behind them, in the final scene.

PROPS:

Props should be kept to minimum. No attempt should be made to use all possible props as would be used in a realistic play. The props used should resonate in the play. For example: MARYJO's guitar and case; SISSY's picture; WHITNEY's liquor bottle, glass, candle;

LEEANN's joint, STEELE's Tet Report; MARTHA's nurse's cap in last scene.

A hand-held period microphone with cord may be used throughout the play in various capacities—both to suggest a real mike (MARYJO scenes) and to connote the impersonality and inhumanness of the world surrounding the women (HEAD NURSE's use of mike in Mass Casualty hospital scene and WHITNEY's use of mike as VA SPOKESPERSON).

Clave sticks, small cylindrical wooden sticks used as percussion musical instruments, popular in Asian countries, are suggested for use in various ways throughout play. They are associated with LEEANN both as her own character, and when she portrays BIEN. They are also used to accentuate movement and mark quick scene shifts (first scenes in ACT II).

Duffle bags, military in style and color, are suggested for each actress, except for MARYJO who should carry a small suitcase. In these bags, actresses should store their personal props and their various costume changes. These bags may be carried with actors from scene to scene—or at least give the audience the illusion of being carried through most of the play by the actresses. The duffles serve the practical need of helping costume and prop requirements. They also lend to the sense of the transiency of the lives of the women both in Vietnam and when they come back, and to the shifting, constantly moving structural style of the play. In some sets, sand bags may be piled around the perimeter of the platforms. These provide perfect areas for hiding props, costumes or ashtrays.

MUSIC:

The songs and lyrics are an integral part of the dramatic through-line of the play. The lyrics become dialogue and MARYJO, as she sings the songs, often is singing the sub-text of the play. To gain an understanding of the kinds of songs the author has intended, producers are urged to contact the author's agent: **Peter Hagen, The Gersh Agency, 41 Madison Avenue, New York, New York, 10010,** to obtain a list of the songs used in the New York production. If producers wish to use any of these songs in performance, they are required to contact the copyright owners directly. It is further suggested that if any additional background music is added to the show such as first act lead-in, etc., that only instrumental music be used. No vocalization or additional lyrics.

COSTUMES:

The women are haunted. Past in the present. Each carries young, idealistic 60's self with her. Costumes reflect this. Two basic costumes (Act I and Act II)—adding/subtracting pieces from scene to scene—are suggested.

The women are dislocated, fragmented. Something about them looks alike. In some way all add up to one woman as all tell the same experience. As if one person split. Possible use of parts of one costume on several characters.

All in variations of same color scheme which darkens as play progresses.

Each character is in one basic costume (such as khaki pants and a shirt) with pieces subtracted and added to it as the play progresses—i.e., vests, scarves, jumpers, hats, jackets: audience should not be cognizant of when actors change garments. There should *not* be the sense of the actors changing costume pieces with every *role* they play. Rather the additions or subtractions should come out of the sense of what the *action of the play* is—camouflage vests added during Tet, the heavy war scene, for example.

Characters also reflect specific disciplines they were in: Navy nurse, Army nurse, Red Cross, civilian. Also reflect regions they come from: MARYJO and Texas, SISSY and midwest, WHITNEY and New England, etc. One costume for THE MAN, added to and subtracted from as with OTHERS.

CHARACTERS:

The six women characters in *A Piece of My Heart* are seen over a 20-year period, from the sixties to the present. Actresses portraying these roles also portray a variety of other roles in the play: military personnel, friends, relatives, acquaintances. The male actor plays all the male roles in the play.

MARTHA   22-42. Strong, self-composed, aura of self-discipline, military bearing. Strong face, American, almost pioneer in feeling.

MARYJO   17-37. Blond, pretty, outgoing, bubbly personality. Texas accent. Sexy; a funny comedienne quality; but sad inside. Must be skillful guitarist and singer.

SISSY   20-40. Sweet, feminine, outgoing. Sense of fun. Also sense of harmony and warmth to personality.

WHITNEY   21-41. Tall, slender, withdrawn, contained. Very aristocratic in bearing and quality. A Vassar graduate.

LEEANN   20-40. Asian or Amerasian. Attractive. Strong, tough, determined in nature. An urban, hip quality to her personality.

STEELE   35-55. Black. Extremely strong, military bearing. Very intelligent, outgoing, great sense of humor. A pragmatist. Southern.

THE AMERICAN MEN—18-60. Tall, very American looking. Versatile actor needed for variety of roles.

Please note:
Mention is made of songs which are *not* in the public domain. Producers of this play are hereby CAUTIONED that permission to produce this play does not include rights to use these songs in production. Producers should contact the copyright owners directly for rights.

ACT I

The recent past.
DUSK. November.
Outside, somewhere near The Wall in Washington, D.C.
MUSIC from band is heard in background: "Under the Double Eagle." MARYJO, WHITNEY, STEELE, MARTHA, SISSY, LEEANN are discovered onstage, staggered positions, back, profile, SISSY front, looking at the sky. THEY wear coats, jackets, etc. THEY will remain onstage throughout the entire play, always listening. MARYJO has guitar, small suitcase near her. OTHERS have military duffle bags.

MALE. (*Voice over.*) COMMENCE FIRE!

(BLAST of ARTILLERY FIRE heard, seen firing into the sky.)

MALE. (*Voice over.*) COMMENCE FIRE!

(BLAST of another ROUND heard and seen. WOMEN look up at the sky.)

MALE. (*Voice over.*) COMMENCE FIRE!

(BLAST heard and seen again. Then a huge round of APPLAUSE, CHEERING, WHISTLING. MUSIC out.)

13

MASTER OF CEREMONIES. (*Voice over.*) Thank you. Thank you ... thank you! We are gathered here today to honor the brave men and women who served so well—and gave so much—

(MARTHA now starts addressing audience.)

MARTHA. (*Smiling a little ruefully.*) I was an Army brat. Martha O'Neill. Dad a career man. Mom a Navy nurse. World War II. I was born at Ft. Benning, grew up at Ft. Bragg. I remember one day in junior high a girlfriend came in crying: her Dad was going to Vietnam. Crying and crying and they sent her home ... must've been around—oh I don't know, 1961 ... so I knew early on about Vietnam. Americans there ... Americans being killed there ... something very wrong there. Back of my mind was: *I* want to go there. Be a Navy nurse and serve my country and protect our men.

(MARYJO turns to audience. MARTHA focuses on Maryjo.)

MARYJO. I was the lead singer and rhythm guitarist in the Sugar Candies All Girl Band. Maryjo Kincaid from Beaumont, Texas. We'd come to LA to get discovered and did Country and Rock and were about seventeen years old and thought we were the livin' end! We hadn't gotten too far *yet*, but one day in '67, an agent told us he could book us—miniskirts and little white go-go boots—to go over and entertain the half a million boys in Vietnam! Well, I was out of my mind! Half a million American boys groovin' on *my* music and lovin' *me* 'cause I'd be liftin' the worries of war right off their shoulders with *my* love for them? "A thousand dollars a month apiece and airfare and all expenses paid," he said. "Oh boy! Book me on!"

(SISSY turns to audience. MARTHA, MARYJO focus on her.)

SISSY. I wanted *out* of Erie, Pennsylvania. I was turning seventeen and I didn't want to rot in Erie, Pennsylvania 'til I was forty years old! I didn't know anything about Vietnam—that wasn't the point. The point was I wasn't into a college scene, I wasn't into demonstrations, I wasn't into anything—Religious family—playing with dolls 'til I was thirteen years old— well, it was still a very sheltered time for girls! My high school counselor said to me: "Well, now, Sissy, what is it you want to be? A nurse, a teacher or a secretary?" "Oh, well sir, a nurse, I guess. I'll help mankind." Now, my biggest problems my first year in Nursing School were, I had no self-control and I couldn't stand to see people in pain! But my instructors said to me: "You don't have a choice here; you just get in there and do as you're told!" So—there's this old man in a coma and I'm supposed to give him a shot of penicillin in his rear-end, and now I am really a wreck because how can I cause this sick old man more pain? But I do it. And the guy immediately comes out of the coma and goes: "Oh my God, where am I?" And I think, "Oh gosh! I did a miracle! I can do anything! I'll join the Army! I'll save the World!"

*(WHITNEY turns to audience. MARTHA, MARYJO,
    SISSY focus on her.)*

WHITNEY. I was graduating from Vassar in primary
education. Provisional Junior League. Sleeves right down
to my elbows. Prim, high proper collars. Already been
offered a boarding school position for the fall term when I
saw a Red Cross form on the Placement Board. I went to
an interview, and they said: "Red Cross has two groups
going overseas early summer. Korea. And Vietnam."
"Well—Saigon's a sophisticated, cosmopolitan city, they
say—diversity of people to meet—all walks of life—and
they speak French! I took my junior year in Paris you
see—besides—it snows in Korea doesn't it? Whereas
Vietnam has this wonderfully warm climate I'm told—" I
went home for the weekend to tell my parents. "But Dad—
Mother—Vietnam will be my year of service. Besides—if
I'm ever going to do anything in my life besides be an old
maid boarding-school teacher, I'd better do it now." It grew
very quiet in the breakfast room. Sunday morning.
Mother's coffee cup rattling in its Dresden saucer. "Look
Whitney—if you insist on running off like this to the ends
of the earth, do be aware you're making a decision of some
consequence. There will be repercussions on your life—not
necessarily for the better—so please, dear—please, do think
it carefully through—" "But Mother, don't you see, I
already have!"

*(CLAVE STICKS sound, three beats. LEEANN turns to
    audience.
MARTHA, MARYJO, SISSY, WHITNEY focus on her.)*

LEEANN. I was anti-war! I hated Nixon! Knew he was a liar and evil! So did my friends! We were hippies—Woodstock, bell bottom jeans, headbands, the long hair, the pot. Then I remember Kennedy going, "What can you do for your country?" Well, I was twenty-one when an Army recruiter comes to my nursing school dressed in her uniform—and she is showing us this wonderful film about the glamour of being an Army nurse and all these gorgeous hospitals all over the world with all this modern equipment—we didn't have zip at my nursing school! And I was very impressed! After the film I ask: "But do nurses *have* to go to Vietnam?" "No!" she goes. "Women *volunteer* for Vietnam." My friends are mostly thinking I am crazy but there are two others who are willing to sign up at any minute and I am thinking: "It is perfect for you Leeann. It will pay for this last year of nursing school—because money for me is very tight—and you can express your feelings about the war by taking care of Nam soldiers when they get *back* from Nam—maybe Hawaii or something. I had been born and raised in New York and am half Italian and half Chinese and went through a lot of prejudice in New York! I wanted to go to Hawaii—where everybody looks like me!

(STEELE turns to audience. OTHERS focus on her.)

STEELE. Well now, I'd been a WAC for almost eighteen years when I decided to go on over to The Nam. First joined up in Jackson, Mississippi where I was born and raised. They asked me: "Steele, what MOS would you like to be?" "Well, I'm a college graduate and have been

teaching music, so I would like to join the Army band."
So, they gave me the *fourth* trombone part to audition
with—and if you know anything about music, you *know*
that is the hard part! The "du-pity-do!" So, I am playing
along with the band—except Commander-in-Chief Warrant
Officer Helen B. Whitehead—you gonna believe that
name?—has made some secret prearranged signal with the
band to stop at a certain point. So all you are hearing is me
going "do-pity-do-pity-do-do-do!" Afterwards she calls me
aside and says, "Oh, sorry about this Steele, but we can't
have any Negroes in the band because you just don't blend
on in!" 1950! My first touch with The American Armed
Services. And how they want you—but they don't really
want you. Anyhow, by 1967 I'd edited an Army
newspaper, run an education center, was a French and
Spanish linguist, a Prisoner of War Interrogator, and was
in Strategic Intelligence. And I knew I was hearing lies
about Vietnam! I'll just go on over there myself I thought.
And maybe my intelligence and experience will be used for
once to save some American lives.

*(Sound of faint WIND CHIMES. LIGHTS shift. WOMEN
    doff coats putting them into duffles as we shift into
    past. MARTHA steps forward.)*

MARTHA. *(To audience.)* August. 1966. I take my
oath, graduate from women's officer school, go to Quonset
Point, Rhode Island for two years. Head nurse in the
Dependents' Unit. Then I tell my folks I'm volunteering
for Vietnam. And they are proud! But not my chief nurse—

(MARTHA goes to STEELE who becomes HEAD NURSE.)

STEELE. (*As HEAD NURSE.*) You're very young Martha! They're looking for people there with experience.

MARTHA. I've got experience! I'm Head Nurse!

STEELE (*As HEAD NURSE.*) Direct *war* experience!

MARTHA. But I've done everything—and I'm really good! And my folks are military. I've been around it all my life!

STEELE. (*As HEAD NURSE.*) I've serious reservations about endorsing this request—

MARTHA. Oh please!

STEELE. (*As HEAD NURSE.*) Well—I—I'm doing it with a *great* deal of hesitation—

MARTHA. (*To audience.*) A Navy Nurse in a War Zone! Like my mother! Glamorous! My deepest childhood dream come true!

SISSY. (*To audience.*) My mother went right down to the Recruiting Office—

(SHE runs to MARTHA who becomes her MOTHER; together THEY hurry to another area where WHITNEY is, WHITNEY becomes RECRUITING OFFICER.)

MARTHA. (*As MOTHER.*) Will my daughter have to go to Vietnam if she joins?

WHITNEY. (*As RECRUITING OFFICER.*) Army nurses *volunteer* for Vietnam. And we have so *many* women wanting to go, madam, we would never even consider a policy like that!

MARTHA. (*To Sissy.*) Good, Sissy! Because what I really want you to do if you're actually going to join, is put in for Germany and meet a doctor and get yourself married and *settle down*!

SISSY. (*To audience.*) My girlfriend and I go for our physicals together—(*SISSY now runs to Leeann as FRIEND, takes Leeann's hand.*) Oh, gosh, kid—I am so nervous—I can't even go in the bottle! Go for me, too!

(LEEANN giggles.)

LEEANN. (*As FRIEND.*) Okay, but I hope I don't have a kidney infection!

SISSY. (*To audience.*) She didn't!

LEEANN. (*As FRIEND. To audience.*) And we passed!

(SISSY and LEEANN now begin running in a circle around the stage, up and down the platforms and ramp.)

LEEANN. (*As FRIEND.*) And ran right out and got a map of Texas! And rented a car.

SISSY. And just flew down the freeways heading south.

LEEANN. (*As FRIEND.*) SOUTH!

SISSY. Ft. Sam Houston! HERE WE COME!

(THEY sit on steps as if in car. MARYJO starts, playing guitar, singing, watching them as does STEELE.
MARYJO sings the first two lines of a popular 40's song desbribing Texas.)

STEELE. (*As if in imaginary bass viola.*)
BOOM, BOOM, BOOM, BOOM

*(MARYJO sings third line of a popular 40's song
describing Texas.)*

SISSY. I'm going to Galveston—first weekend I am
there!
LEEANN. *(As FRIEND.)* I'm going to Mexico and buy
huaraches first weekend I am there!
SISSY. Oh gosh! Let's do something special *every*
weekend we are there!

*(MARYJO and SISSY sing fourth line of a popular 40's
song describing Texas.)*

SISSY/MARYJO/STEELE.
BOOM, BOOM, BOOM, BOOM!

*(SISSY, LEEANN (As FRIEND) MARYJO and STEELE
sing last line of a popular 40's song describing Texas.
(WHITNEY now comes into new area.)*

WHITNEY. *(To audience.)* I report to the Red Cross,
Washington, D.C. For two weeks of training.

(STEELE steps into area; on one side of Whitney.)

STEELE *(As INSTRUCTOR.)* Ladies! You tell
military rank by the stripes on the shirt sleeve. One stripe,
two stripes, three stripes. Is that clear?
WHITNEY. Oh, very clear!

(MARTHA comes into area on other side of Whitney.)

MARTHA. (*As INSTRUCTOR.*) Ladies! You tell the difference between the Army, the Navy, the Air Force and the Marines by color—gray, blue, green, black--and style—button up, button down, cut straight, cut away. Is that clear?

WHITNEY. Oh, very clear!

(*STEELE takes a step closer to Whitney, closing in a little.*)

STEELE. (*As INSTRUCTOR.*) Ladies! There are rules of etiquette—a time to drink, a time not to drink, a way to drink, a brand to drink, a drink to drink. Is that clear?

WHITNEY. Oh, very clear!

(*MARTHA steps closer, closing in more.*)

MARTHA. (*As INSTRUCTOR.*) Ladies! There are proper ways to respond to off-color remarks. There are ways to respond to everything! There are ways to be a young lady worthy of the American Red Cross! Is that clear?

WHITNEY. Oh, very clear!

(*STEELE closes in one more step.*)

STEELE (*As INSTRUCTOR.*) At all times be feminine!

(*MARTHA closes in one more step.*)

MARTHA. *(As INSTRUCTOR.)* Never swear!

STEELE *(As INSTRUCTOR.)* Never be provocative with men!

MARTHA. *(As INSTRUCTOR.)* Because you are a Red Cross girl! *(MARTHA puts arms around Whitney.)*

STEELE. *(As INSTRUCTOR.)* Symbol of Purity!

MARTHA. *(As INSTRUCTOR.)* Goodness and light!

(STEELE puts arm around Whitney on other side.)

STEELE *(As INSTRUCTOR.)* Sister, Mother, Girl-next-door!

MARTHA. *(As INSTRUCTOR.)* *The* All American Girl to every service man you meet!

(WHITNEY, trapped, looks from one to other.)

STEELE. *(As INSTRUCTOR.)* No sexual involvements of any kind!

MARTHA. *(As INSTRUCTOR.)* Forbidden! Against all rules!

STEELE. *(As INSTRUCTOR.)* Now—is that clear?

(WHITNEY, scrunched, looks at audience.)

WHITNEY. Oh, it is very, *very* clear!

(LEEANN now stands, humming, "I'M GOING TO A HOUKI-LAU" and doing hula, as:)

STEELE. *(As OFFICER.)* Now then nurses!

MARTHA. (*As SERGEANT.*) Attention!

(THEY fall into line.)

STEELE. (*As OFFICER.*) This morning we are going to march! Hut-2-3-4! Hut-2-3-4!

(MARYJO begins to strum guitar like drum beat, WHITNEY, MARTHA begin marching in place. SISSY goes center, marching up and downstage. LEEANN continues hula as STEELE comes to her.)

STEELE. Well, well. Welcome to the U.S. Army, Miss Noo Yawk! March!
LEEANN. *March*? I'm a nurse!
STEELE. (*As OFFICER.*) You're an *Army* nurse! And you are going to march!

(LEEANN quickly runs center, starts marching upstage, downstage, alternate move of Sissy's marching path. MARYJO now starts singing.)

MARYJO.
THESE OLD GALS
THEY GO ONE—
THEY GO KNICK KNACK
ON MY THUMB
WITH A KNICK KNACK PADDY WACK
GIVE YOUR DOG A BONE
THESE OLD GALS GO ROLLING HOME

(As THEY are marching.)

SISSY. *(ANOTHER RECRUIT.)* Captain? How come you don't teach us to shoot a gun?
STEELE. *(As OFFICER.)* We do not teach you to shoot weapons or carry weapons because women do not go into combat. *(STEELE now goes over to Leeann.)* March! Miss Noo Yawk—march!

(THEY continue to march.)

LEEANN. Say captain—how come we're always pretending to march through the jungle full of punji sticks?
STEELE *(As OFFICER.)* Because you will probably end up in the jungle, Miss Noo Yawk! In Vietnam! March!
LEEANN. *(Chuckling.)* Vietnam? Oh no, ma'am. My recruiter said Hawaii!

(Guitar strumming stops as STEELE stops marching in place, looks at Leeann as do others. SISSY has joined Whitney, Martha.)

STEELE. *(As OFFICER.)* Hawaii, Miss Noo Yawk?

(OTHERS begin to snicker.)

LEEANN. Honolulu—Waikaki—*(LEEANN does a little hula gesture.)*
STEELE. *(As OFFICER. Suppressing smile.)* Well, you must have been slightly misinformed—

(Moves to OTHERS who shake their heads.)

MARYJO. (*Softly, fearful, moves toward Leeann.*)
WITH A KNICK KNACK PADDY WACK
GIVE YOUR DOG A BONE
THIS OLD GAL GOES ROLLING HOME—

STEELE. (*Comes forward to audience.*) Now there was one thing old Intelligence Officer B. J. Steele did before she went to Vietnam: learned to shoot! Steeley was gonna carry her weapon and know how to fire it over there—make no mistake about that! I learned to strip an M-16. I learned to handle it, fire it, and then I learned to shoot a .45. Got so I could cock *that* thing behind my back! Then I thought: well now, I'm about ready to go over to Vietnam and see what I can see!

(*MARTHA now as SERGEANT, WHITNEY as OFFICER takes a step in new area.*)

MARTHA. (*SERGEANT.*) Attention!

(*ALL rise at attention.*)

WHITNEY. (*As OFFICER.*) All of you have orders for "Southeast Asia."
LEEANN. "Southeast Asia?"
MARTHA. (*As SERGEANT.*) Dismissed!

(*SISSY moves to Leeann.*)

SISSY. They wouldn't even say Vietnam!
LEEANN. I'm going to my head nurse—

(LEEANN turns to STEELE, who is near her.)

STEELE. (*As HEAD NURSE.*) Don't worry, Leeann, the hospitals are safe—miles from the combat zone—

LEEANN. But I'm anti-war.

STEELE. (*As HEAD NURSE.*) So are a lot of the injured boys!

LEEANN. I'll take care of them in Hawaii.

STEELE. (*As HEAD NURSE.*) They're overstaffed there. And you're special. Top of the line. You can make a real contribution for your country in Vietnam.

(LEEANN looks at her.)

STEELE. And the credit will do wonders for your career—after the war—

LEEANN. (*Attracted by this idea.*) Yeah? Yeah.

MARYJO. (*To audience.*) The Sugar Candies' last day—San Francisco—we go to a restaurant on Fisherman's Wharf and the next table knows we're heading to Vietnam to entertain the troops. They buy us drinks and whipped cream desserts. And propose a toast: "To Maryjo Kincaid, the star, and the sweetest, prettiest Sugar Candy all girl band in these United States!"

(THEY are beginning to move toward airplane platform.)

SISSY. (*To audience.*) We buy little black lace bras and bikini panties. A nurse who'd been to Nam says: "Whatever you do bring sexy underwear! A year in boots and fatigues and that dirt and heat and you forget what sex you are."

LEEANN. (*To audience.*) I get to Travis Air Force Base early. I look around. (*SHE now looks at others in astonishment.*

OTHERS. (*Ad-libbing.*) Hi Leeann! Hey—! Hello!

LEEANN. They're from Ft. Sam! Women I *know!*

LEEANN. I'm not special! *Everybody's* here!

(THEY all start climbing onto airplane platform.)

WHITNEY. (*To audience as SHE climbs on airplane platform.*) And they put us on an airplane in little powder blue Red Cross uniforms and dixie cup hats and heels and stockings and girdles!

SISSY. (*To audience.*) And then—for the first time—as we board—they actually announce where they're taking us:

WHITNEY. (*On hand mike.*) Destination Ben Hoa!

(ALL are on platform which has a bench. SOME sit on bench, OTHERS on floor resting on or against their duffle bags.)

MARTHA. And off we go—

(MARYJO begins singing the first verse of an official U.S. Air Force song with guitar.
ALL join in with another verse.)

MARYJO. (*To audience.*) There are just a few women on my plane—two hundred men! And everybody is trying to be sweet ...

SISSY. (*To audience.*) Singing, drinking, playing pinochle, checkers—

WHITNEY. *(To audience.)* And there's this G.I. on my plane coming back from his R&R—

(SOLDIER enters, climbs onto airplane platform.)

SOLDIER. (*To Whitney.*) Well, Doughnut Dollie, you're never gonna make it. There are Viet Cong on the landing fields—

WHITNEY. (*Stunned.*) What?

SOLDIER. The minute the plane lands you'll be shot at—

WHITNEY. Me? That's insane.

SOLDIER. Two bits you don't make it in-country one day—

(MARYJO sings first line of a popular 60's song.)

LEEANN. (*To audience.*) I ask my stewardess for a pillow—she pretends she doesn't hear me—she brings pillows to the men—

(MARYJO sings seond line of the same popular 60's song.)

SISSY. (*To audience.*) My stewardess gives me the same chicken dinner five times going around the world—

(MARYJO sings third line of the same popular 60's song.)

STEELE. *(To audience.)* I'm reading newspapers. The location of American troops from division headquarters down to the platoons. I can do the entire order of battle from my seat on this plane. Now if I know up *here*—the enemy surely *knows* down *there*! So what if we are captured coming down? *(To imaginary captors.)* "I don't know anything about anything! All I am is this expert—on the M-16! I know *why* it jams, *how* it jams, *if* it jams and *when* it jams! Now, you all know yourselves what a horrible old weapon it is! *So* bad, they have to send me over here, just to give advice on how to keep that thing in working order—that's how bad that weapon is!" *(SHE chuckles.)*

MARTHA. *(To audience.)* Then suddenly on my plane it all just quiets down—

(THEY start looking out imaginary plane windows, one by one.)

MARYJO. Nobody talks—
SISSY. Nobody says a word.
LEEANN. Everybody has their noses to the window—
WHITNEY. VIETNAM!
STEELE. Coming in over the coast—
MARTHA. Early morning—
MARYJO. Rice paddies—a village way down there—
LEEANN. Green—my God so green—
MARTHA. How can there be a war way down there?
WHITNEY. Look how beautiful it is—

(Sound of BOOM.)

STEELE. My God!!! Tracers!
MARYJO. Look! There—look there!
LEEANN. Puffs of smoke!
MARTHA. A quick turn up!
WHITNEY. *(Stunned.)* We're being fired on!
SISSY. FIRED ON? I haven't done anything to them!
LEEANN. I'm a nurse!
MARYJO. We take a fast, steep dive—
SISSY. The landing strip—the fire department!
MARTHA. With foam!
STEELE. The treads are off the wheels!
LEEANN. We're landing without treads?
WHITNEY. Look, look down there!
MARYJO. We'll have to run for cover—
SISSY. I'm just this normal girl about to do something not real normal at all!
MARYJO. Like a John Wayne movie! WHEE!!!
STEELE. We come down hard!

(LIGHTS go out.)

MARTHA. HARD!
LEEANN. Night! Blackout! Can't see the runway! Nothing! Dead silent on the plane!
SISSY. But I hear two hundred forty-seven souls breathing on this plane—
WHITNEY. The doors open—

(SPOTLIGHTS and RED AMBULANCE LIGHTS begin flashing.)

MARTHA. Spotlights flashing—

(THEY start climbing off, with their duffle bags.)

MARYJO. I'm so nervous some guy lifts me off the plane. My feet never even touch the steps.

(SOLDIER has climbed off, lifted Maryjo off.)

SISSY. A wave of such heat, such stench hits me— *(SHE turns away, sits again.)* I don't want to go out there—*(STEELE pulls her up.)* But someone pulls me— *(SHE climbs off bench.)*
WHITNEY. Everyone shouting orders to everybody else.

(STEELE now climbs down.)

LEEANN. Vietnamese — everywhere — screaming — shrieking —
STEELE. No! Don't *you* know? That's how their language sounds.

(CLAVE STICKS start beating quickly and ALL scurry around airport to the beat. Then STICKS stop and ALL move slowly around.)

WHITNEY. (*To audience.*) I walk around the airport in Saigon. The Red Cross is supposed to meet me here. I can't find a soul. It's raining. Coming into monsoon season. Raining hard. A limousine comes, takes VIPs from my plane away. School bus, wire on the windows, takes officers—and then, a big, open *cattle* truck pulls up in the rain—the young men I flew with—herded in—

(SHE turns away. MARTHA is near her.)

MARTHA. (*To audience.*) The guy *I* flew with—drank champagne with—God, I don't know if I'll see him again—or what—

(The SOLDIER calls to Martha.)

SOLDIER. Hey—so long Martha—

(MARTHA runs to him.)

(MARYJO with guitar, slowly sings second line, second verse of a popular 60's song.)

MARTHA. So long—

(MARYJO sings third line, second verse of the same popular 60's song.)

(SOLDIER EXITS.)

STEELE. (*To audience.*) I get to some temporary billet. And I'm dirty and wrinkled so I take a shower, start washing, look at my washcloth, and oh my God! It's brown! I'm turnin' *WHITE*? (*SHE bursts out laughing at herself.*) Oh Lord. It's just the dirt of Vietnam.

(*WHITNEY steps to new area.*)

WHITNEY. (*As OFFICER.*) Attention! All new nurses report to North area at once to volunteer for where you want to serve.

(*LEEANN and SISSY move to Whitney.*)

SISSY. Just send me where I'm needed most.
WHITNEY. (*As HEAD NURSE.*) I can't do that, nurse. Volunteer, please.
SISSY. I can't volunteer. I don't know where I am.
WHITNEY. (*As HEAD NURSE.*) The other nurses have managed to figure it out. Please volunteer.

(*LEEANN whispers to Sissy.*)

LEEANN. A G.I. on the plane gave me a list. Vung Tau?
SISSY. (*To Whitney.*) Vung Tau!
LEEANN. (*To Sissy.*) Right on the beach, I hear.
WHITNEY. (*As HEAD NURSE.*) Oh, that's filled. Volunteer again.
LEEANN. (*Whispering.*) Phan Rang.
SISSY. (*To Whitney.*) Phan Rang.
WHITNEY. (*As HEAD NURSE.*) Filled. Volunteer again.

LEEANN. (*To Sissy.*) Cam Ranh Bay?
SISSY. (*To Whitney.*) Cam Ranh Bay.
WHITNEY. (*As HEAD NURSE.*) Sorry! Volunteer again!
LEEANN. That's the bottom of my list.

(*A huge EXPLOSION. SISSY and LEEANN scream, fall to ground hugging each other.*)

WHITNEY. (*As HEAD NURSE.*) Two of you want to stay together I suppose?

(*SISSY and LEEANN are terrified.*)

SISSY. Oh sure!
LEEANN. If we could—

(*WHITNEY sizing them up.*)

WHITNEY. (*As HEAD NURSE.*) How about Cu Chi?
LEEANN and SISSY. Cu Chi?
WHITNEY. (*As HEAD NURSE.*) I can keep you together—for a while—*if* you *volunteer* for Cu Chi—
SISSY. All right—fine—
SISSY and LEEANN. We *volunteer* for Cu Chi!
WHITNEY. (*As HEAD NURSE.*) C-130's loading. There. Get on! Fast!

(*WHITNEY stands, motions toward bench where SISSY and LEEANN run.*
SISSY and LEEANN climb on bench, as SOLDIER enters, sits on bench.)

SISSY. (*To audience.*) We pile in and it is all men. (*To Soldier.*) Hey, who are you?

SOLDIER. The spray boys!

LEEANN. What's *that* mean?

SOLDIER. We spray the area with heavy chemical spray—to kill weeds.

SISSY. (*Surprised.*) Weeds?

SOLDIER. So Charley can't hide in the jungle!

(*SISSY looks at him.*)

(*MARYJO comes forward as SOLDIER exits. MARYJO circles downstage area.*)

MARYJO. (*To audience.*) I live out of my suitcase. On the road! Three shows a day! Up in a C-130 to Danang, down to Marble Mountain in a chopper, back up to Danang at night. I'm at the airport hours, days—or I sleep in a military truck—or officers' quarters they give up for us—or a trailer pulled up close. My first show is at the USO club up north. And we are wall to wall Marines! And they are *so* cute! They are *so* adorable! With those great big eyes and their shaven heads and their green fatigues! I'm just falling in love with every single one of them at first sight!

(*MARYJO comes onto platform in new area. SOLDIER sits nearby. MARTHA, SISSY, STEELE, LEEANN start gathering around her as her BACK-UPS.*)

WHITNEY. (*To audience*.) We help the USO girls serve eight hundred hot dogs and shakes the night of the first show!

MARYJO. I come right on stage with my signature song—

WHITNEY. (*Speaking into hand mike*.) And here they are—for your listening pleasure—The Sugar Candies All Girl Band with MARYJO. Let's hear it for The Sugar Candies All Girl Band!

(*SHE holds hand mike up for Maryjo as SOLDIER and OTHERS clap, whistle, stomp their feet for her. As SHE sings a country-rock song of the 60's, BACK-UPS do "sixties movements."*
SOLDIER, BACK-UPS clap, yell, whistle loudly, then it dies down.)

MARYJO. (*Softly*.) Thank you! I love you all! Every single one—

WHITNEY. (*Moves to new area. To audience*.) I live in the city—lovely villa—except it's right on Prostitute Row—(*SHE laughs softly*.) Several Red Cross women to share with. A housekeeper, Bien, whom I *love!* Oh I like *all* the Vietnamese ... But not the Vietnamese Army Guards outside our house at night—ARVN guards they call them. Protecting us, they say. But the way they look at me—I don't know—something seems fishy to me—

(*MARTHA steps forward.*)

MARTHA. (*To audience*.) The hospital is a series of Quonset huts—I'm assigned to the night shift.

(WHITNEY as HEAD NURSE. leads her from platform to platform, explaining.)

WHITNEY. (*As HEAD NURSE.*) Captain, as you can see, the Quonset huts are divided into orthopedics, surgery, medicine, intensive care—and then we have our pre-op, x-ray, post-op, recovery and the offices. Now, all these huts are lined up, one after the other—and between them please notice we have bunkers.

MARTHA. (*Surprised.*) Bunkers?

WHITNEY. (*As HEAD NURSE.*) In case of a rocket attack. Then we're on what we call "red alert."

MARTHA. "Red Alert?"

WHITNEY. (*As HEAD NURSE.*) "Red Alert" means you are in immediate danger—a direct rocket hit. Or a sapper attack. When the enemy penetrates our perimeter. If you're off-duty you crawl immediately into a bunker. If you're on duty, put on flak jackets, helmets, and put the mattresses *over* all your patients, then take cover yourself, while someone guards the door.

MARTHA. (*Stunned.*) I see—

WHITNEY. (*As HEAD NURSE.*) We're on "Red Alert" most of the time—

MARTHA. I see.

(THEY are winding around in a circle on the stage from platform to platform.)

WHITNEY. (*As HEAD NURSE.*) Now here, on the wards, since you will have a lot of corpsmen to assist you,

you will be responsible, Captain, for three hundred to three hundred and fifty patients in all. And, as supervisor you will be expected to care for the sickest patients yourself.

MARTHA. (*Staggered.*) Three hundred and fifty patients?

WHITNEY. (*As HEAD NURSE.*) Night duty is the hardest, of course. People die at night. And wounded people, Captain, get very frightened at night. They moan, they cry out—here—here—this way please—

MARTHA. (*To audience.*) She was right—my chief nurse stateside—I don't have the experience for this—

(THEY stop by a bench.)

WHITNEY. (*As HEAD NURSE.*) Now, your job will include all the routine things, of course—reading the charts, checking the IVs, the dressings, the casts—

MARTHA. (*To audience.*) Suction! Respirators! Infusing fluids! Catheters! Tubes! Drains! I don't know what I'm looking at! I can't find the patient here!

WHITNEY. (*As HEAD NURSE.*) Don't think about it in that way! What you must do is focus on the facts. And write the data down.

MARTHA. But I've never seen anything like this in my life!

WHITNEY. (*As HEAD NURSE.*) Captain please! Just keep on checking the charts, the dressings, the IVs and the casts. Think only of what you're checking. Shut out all the rest! Build a psychological wall! Now, come on Captain—we'll go to the next ward—

(SHE starts walking, MARTHA trailing.)

MARTHA. (*To audience*.) Please God—don't let there be so many horrible things wrong on the next ward—

WHITNEY. (*As HEAD NURSE*.) Here are the more seriously injured men—our intensive care patients—come along—

MARTHA. (*Stops*.) I can't take anymore!

(*WHITNEY turns to regard her*.)

WHITNEY. (*As HEAD NURSE*.) Stuff it, Captain! Behind that wall! Or you will never function or be of use!

MARTHA. But there are so *many* injuries—and the *kinds* of injuries—and the—

WHITNEY. (*As HEAD NURSE. Interrupting*.) The Medical Corps motto is: "Conserve the Fighting Strength!" Your work is to patch up the soldier so he can get back to the battle field—

MARTHA. Yes, ma-am—

WHITNEY. (*As HEAD NURSE*.) Keep walking—briskly—ward to ward to ward. Walk!

MARTHA. (*Starting to briskly walk ahead of WHITNEY as THEY march one way, turn, march back again*.) Yes—I—I'll just have to keep walking along—

WHITNEY. (*As HEAD NURSE*.) Walk and don't think! Write and don't think! Don't think! Don't think! Don't let those thoughts come through that wall! Stay behind your wall!

(*WHITNEY and MARTHA continue to march across stage, turn, march back again as:*)

MARTHA. (*To audience.*) I volunteered.
MARYJO. (*Singing softly, looking at Martha.*)
KNICK KNACK PADDY WACK
MARTHA. (*To audience.*) I asked for it—
MARYJO.
GIVE YOUR DOG A BONE
MARTHA. (*To audience.*) I have to come through somehow—
MARYJO.
THIS OLD GAL GOES ROLLIN' HOME

(*SISSY comes forward.*)

SISSY. (*To audience.*) My first day at the hospital they had a mass casualty—

(*LEEANN comes forward.*)

LEEANN. (*To audience.*) I was in Emergency—

(*MARTHA comes forward.*)

MARTHA. (*To audience.*) Post-op—
SISSY. (*To audience.*) Pre-op—
LEEANN. (*To audience.*) Surgery—a circulating nurse—

(*MARYJO picks up hand mike, stands on high platform.*)

MARYJO. (*As VOICE on intercom.*) This is Receiving. There is a mass casualty coming in. All doctors, nurses, corpsmen able to leave your lines please report at once to Emergency. I repeat: mass casualty is coming in. All doctors, nurses, corpsmen please report—I repeat, a mass casualty—I repeat—

(MARYJO keeps repeating as WHITNEY [NURSE], STEELE [NURSE] go to high platform with MARYJO. LEEANN, SISSY, MARTHA, downstage center area speaking to each other.)

SISSY. I don't know how to describe it—
LEEANN. I was just thrown into it—
MARTHA. Thrown!

(THEY stop, standing huddled together.)

MARYJO. (*Voice over.*) All *new* nurses! Please report to first group at the left for Orientation please! All *new* nurses report! *Please!*

(SHE keeps repeating now under dialogue. MARTHA, SISSY, LEEANN run up to a platform.)

MARTHA. They tried to show us where the equipment was.
SISSY. Bandages—
LEEANN. Sterilizers—
SISSY. Catheters.
LEEANN. IVs.
MARTHA. Medications—
LEEANN. But there's so much to remember—

(Sound of CHOPPERS begins.)

   SISSY. It's getting terribly confusing in here!

(SOUND grows louder.)

   MARYJO. *(Voice over.)* Helicopters coming in!
Attention Emergency! Helicopters coming in!

(THEY run toward SOUND, back to downstage area.)

   LEEANN. Coming! Coming!

(SOUND louder.)

   SISSY. Closer—closer—

(SOUND of landing.)

   SISSY. Landing!
   MARTHA. Wind—dust flying in my face—
   SISSY. Corpsmen running to the chopper, getting
injured men—

*(SISSY, LEEANN now carry bench up to another
   platform, MARTHA coming with them.)*

   LEEANN. Running back with stretchers—
   MARTHA. Leaving men on metal beds—
   LEEANN. Across sawhorses—

("BEEP" heartbeat sound of CARDIOMETER begins.)

MARTHA. On the floor—

(G.I. enters, stands before them center stage, back to audience. THEY freeze.)

LEEANN. (*Looking at him.*) Holy SHIT!
SISSY. He's got no legs!
MARTHA. Gone!
SISSY. Thighs down!

(LEEANN, then SISSY, then MARTHA start down from platform toward G.I., looking at him.)

LEEANN. So much blood!
MARTHA. Mud!
LEEANN. Green fatigues soaked!
SISSY. Funky!
MARTHA. Brown gauze soaked bandages—
MARYJO. (*On hand mike.*) Doctors and nurses! Take your posts please! Doctors and nurses *please*!
LEEANN. The doctors and nurses are doing ten thousand things!

(MARYJO's announcement continues. WHITNEY and STEELE come on high platform in front of Maryjo.)

WHITNEY. (*As HEAD NURSE. To new nurses.*) We need IVs. We need all the uniforms off!

STEELE. (*As HEAD NURSE. To new nurses.*) We need name, rank, serial number on each one!

MARTHA. But look! Blood is spurting up!

WHITNEY. (*As HEAD NURSE. To new nurses.*) We need IVs and uniforms off!

SISSY. BLOOD IS SPURTING UP!

STEELE. (*As HEAD NURSE.*) We need name, rank, serial number please!

MARTHA. (*To audience.*) I can't move! I can't talk! I can't do anything!

SISSY. (*To audience.*) I can't even look at the second stretcher 'cause I'm still stunned by the first.

STEELE. (*As HEAD NURSE. To Leeann.*) Nurse! Move! Go with that *experienced* nurse! (*To Sissy.*) Move! Nurse! Go to Post-Op! Move!

WHITNEY. (*As HEAD NURSE. To Martha.*) Nurse! Pre-Op! Move!

MARTHA. I can't move!

LEEANN. Can't think!

SISSY. I don't know what to do!

MARTHA. Amputations—

LEEANN. Burn cases—

SISSY. Tracheotomies—

MARTHA. G.I.s—

LEEANN. Vietnamese—

SISSY. Women—and a *child*—

MARTHA. Part of me is saying:

LEEANN. Jesus Christ! Just look at this!

SISSY. The other part says:

LEEANN. What's your problem?

WHITNEY and STEELE. (*As HEAD NURSE. To Leeann.*) Move!

MARYJO. Doctors and nurses take your posts please! Mass casualty coming in!

SISSY. I thought they'd orient me somehow—oh God!

STEELE. (*As HEAD NURSE. To Leeann.*) Nurse, start the IV! Nurse!

LEEANN. I can't! Doctors did it at home! I don't know how!

STEELE. (*As HEAD NURSE.*) START THE IV!

LEEANN. Then show me! For God's sake show me how!

STEELE. (*As HEAD NURSE.*) With twenty men watching? You have to have their confidence!

LEEANN. By making them guinea pigs? SHOW ME WHAT TO DO!

STEELE. (*As HEAD NURSE.*) Get over there! I'll *tell* you what to do. Then you just get in there and do it nurse! *CAN DO*!

LEEANN. *CAN DO*!

WHITNEY. (*As HEAD NURSE.*) Here! Nurse? Cut off this patient's clothes! He's very bad! Hold his head.

SISSY. (*To audience.*) And I turn, and I look at this patient—

LEEANN. (*To audience.*) And half this soldier's face is gone!

(*MARYJO stops announcement. G.I. turns front to audience.*)

SISSY. It's okay, I'm here—I'm right beside you ... His name is Jimmy. And he's *wide awake*! Jimmy? You're not alone—I'm here—

JIMMY. (*To audience*.) Where?

SISSY. Here, Jimmy. Here—

WHITNEY. (*As HEAD NURSE*.) Cut off his clothes! Take off his boots!

SISSY. (*To audience*.) So I do.

LEEANN. (*To audience*.) And his foot is in his boot!

WHITNEY. (*As HEAD NURSE*.) Draw four tubes of blood, type-cross him, get it over to the lab! *Move*!

(SISSY starts to go.)

JIMMY. (*To audience*.) No! Don't go! Stay!

SISSY. It's just across the hall—I'll be back—I have an order to go!

JIMMY. (*To audience*.) No—

(SHE starts away again. "FLATLINER" sound on CARDIOMETER begins.)

MARTHA. (*To Sissy*.) He's dead!

WHITNEY. (*As HEAD NURSE*.) Cover him! Move on! Move on!

LEEANN. He knew he was going—he knew—

SISSY. I should've stayed—oh God, I should've held his hand—

WHITNEY. (*As HEAD NURSE*.) Next patient! *Move on*!

SISSY. My first patient—my first day—

MARTHA. Jimmy!

SISSY. I should've stayed—

LEEANN. I'm holding his boot with his foot in it—

SISSY. Oh God!

LEEANN. I'm going to pass out—
MARTHA. I fall across him—
LEEANN. Trying to deep breathe—trying to stay with the program—trying—
SISSY. Jimmy—

(SOLDIER exits.)

STEELE. (*As HEAD NURSE.*) Take that part in the boot and these other parts in that plastic bag—haul it all out of here—put it in the drum—throw gas on it and burn it up!
WHITNEY. (*As HEAD NURSE. To all on hand mike.*) All right. *New* nurses, you are relieved! Your shift is done.
STEELE. (*As HEAD NURSE. On hand mike.*) Go to your hooches now.
WHITNEY. Relax! Have fun!

(THEY stand stunned, unable to move.)

MARYJO. (*With guitar, slowly.*)
KNICK KNACK PADDY WACK
GIVE YOUR DOG A BONE
THESE OLD GALS GO ROLLING HOME!

(As MARYJO sings, THEY slowly move to new area, sinking down on floor, benches. WHITNEY and STEELE move into new area too, sitting.)

WHITNEY. (*To audience.*) Well, I started drinking over in Vietnam. (*SHE pours a drink, then sips it.*)

MARTHA. (*To audience*.) A lot. Spent most of my spare time in fact hitting the old booze bottle—

MARYJO. (*Joins them, reclining on bench with her guitar*.) And playing my guitar—

WHITNEY. To make it all go away for a while—

MARYJO. (*Singing and strumming*.)
NINETY NINE BOTTLES OF BEER ON THE WALL—
NINETY NINE BOTTLES OF BEER—

SISSY. Well, you couldn't drink beer while you were working—then you just kept smoking cigarettes and drinking cokes—eighteen, twenty, twenty-five cokes. Every break you got! But on your day off—

MARYJO.
IF ONE OF THOSE BOTTLES
SHOULD HAPPEN TO FALL—

STEELE. I am here to tell you we consumed an enormous amount of booze in Vietnam.

MARYJO.
NINETY EIGHT BOTTLES
OF BEER ON THE WALL!

(*MARTHA stands. SHE is smoking joint.*)

LEEANN. Well—the corpsmen usually had pot—so we all did a little pot!

MARTHA. (*Laughing*.) A *little*!

LEEANN. But I only did it with other people! (*SHE giggles.*)

STEELE. Tell it to the Marines!

(*THEY all laugh. MARTHA hands LEEANN joint.*)

LEEANN. Well, *one* person at least—
WHITNEY. You?
LEEANN. All right! One of the things I did *with* people or *without* was *get stoned* on a *lot* of pot!

(THEY laugh.
MARYJO sings first line of a popular 60's song with references to pot.)
LEEANN takes big toke of joint, exhales slowly as WHITNEY rises.)

WHITNEY. We used to go to these marvelous Basque restaurants and stay 'til the wee hours drinking French champagne—whole gang of us—Red Cross gals—military guys—officers—
MARYJO.
VIVE LA, VIVE LA, VIVE L'AMOUR!

(WHITNEY begins to dance to the music.)

WHITNEY. *(Singing.)*
VIVE LA, VIVE LA, VIVE L'AMOUR!
MARYJO and WHITNEY.
VIVE LA, VIVE LA, VIVE L'AMOUR!
WHITNEY. I remember one night we were all pretty mellow and a Marine gave me a bunch of things on a string—and I say: "Oh, gosh, apricots for me! Here I am in a war zone and you got me apricots!" And he goes: "Those are Gook ears ma'am!"

(THEY all laugh.)

EVERYONE.
VIVE LA COMPAGNIE!
STEELE. I had me this nice, nice gentleman colonel friend—and everyday he'd bring me a quart of Crown Royal and drink with me for a while—
MARYJO. I had a date with an officer—wonderful guy. And we waited out a storm together once, drinking Beaujolais. Typhoon down on the shore—and we just made us a pizza in his electric skillet, sat ourselves on the patio, feet up, sipping wine and watching the rain and the wind below—oh Lord, we made some good love—waiting out that storm—
LEEANN. (*To audience.*) I meet a guy in one of the wards—

(HANK enters, starts moving across stage.)

LEEANN. Hank? (*SHE rises, moving slowly towards him. Looking at him.*) Then later he sees me going to the hooch—and he's with this bunch of guys—in jeans—T-shirts—and boonie hats—

(MARYJO rises, begins strumming romantic sixties melody. Slowly, softly.)

HANK. (*Seeing Leeann, stopping.*) Hey—Leeann?
LEEANN. (*Moves toward him. Laughing.*) Hey! You are looking like you just got off a plane from Woodstock! Who *are* you anyhow?

HANK. Dog scout unit—other side of the compound—
you gotta come on over to our place, Leeann—black
lights, posters—just like home.

LEEANN. Yeah?

HANK. When you get off?

LEEANN. Now!

HANK. Come on—walk you over—walk you home—
you'll be safe—I'll take care of you, okay?

*(HANK holds out his hand, LEEANN takes it. THEY
circle 'round the stage.)*

LEEANN. *(To audience.)* And we walk across the
compound together—And come to find out—

HANK. *(To Leeann.)* We both like—

HANK and LEEANN. *(To each other.)* Led Zeppelin!

HANK. Well all right! Wow!

LEEANN. And we're both from the East—

HANK and LEEANN. New—

LEEANN. York!

HANK. Jersey!

(THEY laugh.)

LEEANN. *(To audience.)* Wow! I'm getting very
comfortable with this Hank!

*(THEY come to area where others are. Some sit, dance,
stand. Some smoke pot. Zeppelin MUSIC begins, loud.
PSYCHEDELIC LIGHTS now in this area flashing.)*

LEEANN. We go into the hooch—and Led Zeppelin is loud! *LOUD*!

(HANK is holding Leeann's hands at arms' length.)

LEEANN. And there are all these incredible day-glo posters all over the walls—the ceiling—and oh God! Psychedelic lights!

(SHE is looking at ceiling. HE spins her around.)

LEEANN. And nobody is talking WAR! Nobody is talking MEDICINE! They are talking—
MARYJO. Food—real good food—
MARTHA. Music—real good music—
STEELE. And home—way down home—
HANK. Somewhere I can go fishin' man!

(LEEANN sinks down on bench, HANK on floor, head in her lap.)

WHITNEY. Massachusetts has lakes. You can fish—swim—and eat! Super restaurants.
MARYJO. (*Ordering.*) I'll have me a cowboy-cut ribeye, rare; french fries, crisp, on the side; half order of barbecue chicken and ribs; one chili dog; a cheese and bean enchilada, one pork burrito; a Dad's Root Beer, twelve ounce size; and a double hot fudge walnut sundae with peach ice cream.
STEELE. Girl, you're gonna be sick for days.
HANK. Know my first choice in cars? Benz. (*HANK takes a yellow ribbon from his pocket.*) Second? Porche.

Third? Red Thunderbird. (*HE ties the ribbon on Leeann's ponytail.*)

LEEANN. You think you're gonna be in league for a Benz?

HANK. God damn right I am!

LEEANN. (*To audience.*) Stupid, wonderful talk!

(*MUSIC now shifts to slow Charlie Parker jazz/blues.*)

MARYJO. PARTY TIME!!

HANK. Come on ... Let's dance.

(*HE and LEEANN now rise and begin slow-dancing to music, very close. Romantically.*)

MARYJO. (*Moving slowly, a little; to music.*) God, you G.I.s know how to party! You infantrymen!

SISSY. (*Thinking about this.*) What I love are the stand-downs—your *off-limits* parties! We ride on trucks that take supplies to your unit—and you hide us! In blankets! And sneak us right through the gates and into your unit! Wow!

STEELE. I like your formal parties most—(*SHE is thinking about this. Luxuriating in the mood of the music.*) You offer to *fly* us to your officers' club—and we get all dressed up and away we fly with you—way up over the compound—guns on both sides of the plane protecting us—

MARTHA. (*Moves to the music sensuously.*) And we bring our swimsuits—because what we want most of all is to get off our sweaty clothes and swim with you—115 degrees of heat and the water so cool on our skin.

MARYJO. Only three feet of water—and plastic sides on the pool—and bugs—But there's Texas barbecue.

WHITNEY. (*Who has been drinking through scene.*) And good liquor—

STEELE. And steaks—

MARYJO. Oh God, it's party time—

(MUSIC fades out. HANK and LEEANN stop dancing. LEEANN takes out small diary, looking at Hank.)

LEEANN. Sunday the 14th. Hank is ringing my chimes!

(LEEANN sits, opening diary. HANK crosses away to another area, sitting on bench.)

LEEANN. Like his scene! Go to his hooch depressed, exhausted. One hour and I am feeling good. Black lights hypnotizing me. Here—in Vietnam—

WHITNEY. (*Steps forward. To audience.*) I fell in love. Bruce. A pilot. But I wouldn't sleep with him because it was against the rules. Now wasn't that something when they said Red Cross girls charged a fee? Bruce was flying a mission next morning and we were at the officers' club when he gets very drunk—

(SHE goes to BRUCE who sits on bench with empty bottle.)

BRUCE. I'm not coming back tomorrow.

WHITNEY. What?
BRUCE. I'm gonna get another scotch—

(HE rises, starts staggering out. SHE takes him by the arm.)

WHITNEY. Look—Bruce—let's go—

(Tries to lead him other direction. HE breaks free.)

BRUCE. Where? Your place? "Oh Brucie of course not!" I'm gettin' another scotch—*(Starts out again.)*
WHITNEY. Come on—you need to sleep it off—
BRUCE. Sleep it off where?

(WHITNEY looks around at OTHERS listening.)

WHITNEY. Bruce, I just can't—
BRUCE. God damn cock tease! "Oh Brucie, want a doughnut? Let's hold hands!" Shit! Friggin' Doughnut Dollie! You shouldn't be in a fuckin' war! Now will you just get yourself the fuck off my back and out of my life?

(WHITNEY tries to take him away. HE pushes her off.)

BRUCE. Let go of me! *(HE smashes empty bottle against bench, breaking it.)* I never want to see you again! *(HE staggers from area, holding neck of broken bottle in his hand.)*

WHITNEY. (*To audience.*) And he didn't. Next morning he got shot down. And I never got involved—again. (*SHE sits, turning away.*)

LEEANN. (*To audience, writing in diary.*) Friday the 28th. Hank tells me he's leaving. His time is short enough that he is going home in *days*—from Vietnam—

SISSY. It's the 4th of July when I meet Bill. In August he and his buddy Rory come to get me for a stand-down—

(*As SHE speaks SHE climbs up with RORY to sit on back of a truck [bench].*)

SISSY. And we get on the truck and are riding along—drinking Wild Turkey—passing the bottle back and forth—when Bill has to go to the john. We stop—he jumps down—trots to the bushes, and—

(*Sound of EXPLOSION. SISSY screams.*)

RORY. He stepped on a mine!

(*SISSY jumps off bench. RORY grabs her arm pulling her back up.*)

RORY. Get back up! *Get up!*

(*HE pulls her up, holds her there, SISSY straining to get back down.*)

SISSY. Bill's dead? Let me go! I have to go get him!! Bill's dead?

RORY. The detail will be back. The whole place is mined. (*Leans forward as if to talk to driver.*) Steve? Let her roll! GO! GO!

(*RORY pushes SISSY down on bench.*)

SISSY. He's gone? Bill's gone?—
RORY. Drink some of this—here—(*HE offers her flask.*)

(*RORY is terrified too.*)

SISSY. (*Getting hysterical.*) I'm the only woman here—if it wasn't for me he wouldn't have had to get off and go in the bushes—he wouldn't have—
RORY. Stop it!
SISSY. But if it wasn't for me—
RORY. (*Shaking her.*) Stop it! That kind of shit thinking gets nobody nowhere! Now take a drink and SHUT THE SHIT UP! (*HE offers her flask, holding her very close.*)
LEEANN. (*Looking at diary.*) Tuesday. The 8th. Hank's missing. They took his day-glo posters down. Hank's gone. (*SHE looks up. To audience.*) And I think I am going to die—here in Vietnam—

(*STEELE rises.*)

STEELE. (*As HEAD NURSE.*) Nurse? (*SHE comes to Leeann.*) Is that a ribbon in your hair? Get it off! And never wear that reeking perfume on duty again! And put your cap back on! Straight.

(LEEANN removes ribbon, STEELE goes to another area.)

LEEANN. Because I look like a woman? Act like a woman? Want to look good for my guys on the Ward? I mean, they are *dying*! And in the middle of *dying*—they go: "God, you smell like roses!"—*if* they've still got a nose! Or, "God, you look beautiful!," *if* they've still got eyes! So—you think I'm not going to wear perfume on the Ward? You think I'm not going to wear a yellow ribbon in my hair? *(SHE puts ribbon back on.)*

(SISSY and MARYJO together in another area move forward.)

SISSY. *(To Maryjo.)* You know, I always think no matter what you're going through the guys have got it worse—so we have to be there for them after hours— partying, socializing—

(MARYJO moves to bench, sits. SISSY following, sitting beside her on ground.)

MARYJO. I don't think that anymore—when I first got here—I thought that—but I learned—I mean, sex is a physical urgency for them—and I love them—

(MARYJO and SISSY freeze their positions as WHITNEY sitting in adjacent area, starts drinking, addressing audience.)

WHITNEY. (*To audience*.) Stay in your room drinking alone and they think you're mistress for a married doctor— or Lesbian for another Red Cross girl—(*WHITNEY freezes*.)

MARYJO. (*To Sissy*.) But I have to protect *myself*— survival level! Because, I mean they project on to me—

SISSY. (*To Maryjo*.) Huh?

MARYJO. (*To Sissy*.) I'm up there singing—and they're seeing me—thinking about me—in detail— physically—

(*MARYJO and SISSY freeze*.)

WHITNEY. (*To audience*.) I don't care what anybody thinks anymore. My personal life is my affair. (*WHITNEY freezes*.)

MARYJO. (*To Sissy*.) But if it gives them something they need—to keep them going—I don't care. And they're gentlemen—mostly—

(*SISSY and MARYJO freeze. MARTHA [JANE] in Whitney's area. SHE now turns, comes to Whtiney*.)

MARTHA. (*As JANE*.) Whitney?
WHITNEY. Jane?

(*MARTHA sits beside Whitney*.)

MARTHA. (*As JANE*.) You left—
WHITNEY. I—I get migraines ...

MARTHA. (*As JANE.*) I came back—
WHITNEY. I had to get out of there—
MARTHA. (*As JANE.*) You were gone—

(*MARTHA and WHITNEY freeze.*)

SISSY. (*To Maryjo.*) Dancing, drinking, talking—the
soldiers are always polite—We're just their friends—
"Round-Eye American Girl from home!"

(*SISSY and MARYJO freeze.*)

MARTHA. (*As JANE. To Whitney.*) You have
anything to relieve the pain? Besides aspirin?
WHITNEY. (*To Martha.*) Nothing relieves the pain—

(*WHITNEY looks at Martha. THEY freeze.*)

MARYJO. (*To Sissy.*) Look, the men have respect for
you. You're Army—there're rules—I'm different—I mean
after the gigs—if we stay overnight where they are—
SISSY. (*To Maryjo.*) What are you talking about?
MARYJO. (*To Sissy.*) Some—some crazy stuff's
happened—stuff that never would've happened at home—

(*MARYJO and SISSY freeze.*)

(*MARTHA is behind. WHITNEY has begun massaging
  her shoulders.*)

MARTHA. (*As JANE. To Whitney.*) I could get you
something. I know some nurses.

WHITNEY. (*To Martha.*) Yeah?

MARTHA. (*As JANE. To Whitney.*) To take the edge off—

WHITNEY. (*To Martha.*) Wouldn't it be wonderful—to take the edge off—

(THEY freeze.)

SISSY. (*To Maryjo.*) What are you talking about?

MARYJO. But I wasn't forced ... not really ...

(MARYJO and SISSY freeze.)

WHITNEY. (*Shifting slightly away.*) Look—let's go back to the party, shall we?

MARTHA. (*As JANE.*) No. Let's just stay here.

WHITNEY. Here?

(MARTHA and WHITNEY freeze.)

MARYJO. (*To Sissy.*) A coupla weeks ago we got stranded—up the coast near Nha Trang—then the grunts—but they apologized—well, one apologized—

SISSY. (*To Maryjo.*) Oh God!

MARYJO. (*To Sissy.*) It—it doesn't matter—

SISSY. (*To Maryjo.*) Of course it matters—

MARYJO. (*To Sissy.*) Whole place is so unreal it doesn't matter—no consequences—nothing matters—

(MARYJO and SISSY freeze.)

MARTHA. (*As JANE.*) Yes. Let's just stay here together, okay?

WHITNEY. Okay.

(Pause. WHITNEY and MARTHA freeze.)

SISSY. (*To Maryjo.*) Ever talk to the chaplain?

MARYJO. (*To Sissy.*) *I'm* not religious—

SISSY. (*To Maryjo.*) You could lead out in the choir I bet—Sundays?

MARYJO. (*To Sissy.*) *Me*?

SISSY. (*To Maryjo.*) Something to hang on to— Maryjo?

(SISSY and MARYJO freeze.)

WHITNEY. (*To Martha.*) Okay.

(MARTHA and WHITNEY embrace, freeze.)

(MARYJO rises, takes a step away, begins singing softly, tentatively, trying to find solace, strength in the song, trying to hang on: "Fairest Lord Jesus.")

MARYJO.
FAIR ARE THE MEADOWS
FAIRER THE WOODLANDS
ROBED IN FLOWERS OF BLOOMING SPRING
JESUS IS FAIRER
JESUS IS PURER
HE MAKES OUR SORROWING SPIRITS SING ...

SISSY. (*Comes forward. To audience.*) What finally broke me on duty on the Ward was carolling. At Christmas time.

(*MARYJO begins walking into new area, singing a popular Christmas song with guitar.*)

MARYJO.
JOLLY OLD ST. NICHOLAS
LEAN YOUR EAR THIS WAY
CHRISTMAS EVE IS COMING SOON
HERE'S WHAT I HAVE TO SAY:
ALL. (*As THEY come into new area where G.I. sits on a bench on a platform. ALL beginning to gather near him.*)
JOHNNY WANT A PAIR OF SKATES
SUZY WANTS A SLED
BILLY WANTS A PICTURE BOOK
YELLOW, BLUE AND RED
STEELE. (*Hanging a string of Christmas tree lights somewhere on set near G.I.*) All through the hospitals we decorate—Christmas trees and mistletoe and holly wreaths—every single ward in Vietnam—
WHITNEY. (*Lighting a votive candle and placing it on floor near G.I.*) The USO girls go with us right into the field with a turkey dinner for every guy—
STEELE. And we bring presents to the wards—
WHITNEY. And write Christmas cards—
STEELE. And comfort the boys—

(*THEY are all around G.I. now.*)

MARYJO. (*To G.I.*) Hey, soldier, beautiful scar you're gonna have—

WHITNEY. (*To G.I.*) A terrific souvenir from Nam.

STEELE. And then we play a game—

WHITNEY. "Dear Santa"—where every guy reads out:

G.I. (*To audience.*) Dear Santa! I want a draft-dodging, anti-war demonstrator in my stocking please! Wrap him up and send him *here*. 'Cause I ain't got no leg to put in that stocking anymore myself. Just stick *him* in instead.

WHITNEY. And then we hook up telephone lines—

STEELE. (*On phone.*) Hi Son! Merry Christmas. Happy New Year too, Son! Take care! You hear?

G.I. (*On phone.*) Mom—is that *you*? *Mom*! Oh God, *Mom*!? It's *ME!* Your son, Jerome. Merry Christmas Mom!

MARYJO. And then *we* entertain. Dancing down the aisles.

(*SISSY, MARTHA, STEELE, WHITNEY, LEEANN form line behind MARYJO. THEY dance and sing a popular Christmas song, coming down stairs near G.I.'s platform.*
G.I. applauds, whistles. SISSY and LEEANN step into new area. Sit.)

SISSY. We get picked to go to the Bob Hope Christmas Show! (*Looking around, then to Leeann.*) Gee, there aren't many other girls here!

LEEANN. We're lucky! God! We just lucked out!

SISSY. They've got us all roped *off* from the guys though—

LEEANN. They're grunts—just out of the field—they'll send 'em right back tonight after the show.

SISSY. And they haven't seen a woman for weeks, huh?

(G.I. flashes camera from his area.)

SISSY. What's that?

G.I. *(Calling from distance.)* Just wanted your picture ma'am—to have with me in the fields—

SISSY. *(To Leeann.)* I don't like that. It shakes me somehow. Why'd he do that for?

(MARYJO sings "Away In a Manger" moving into area close to G.I. who lies on a bench.)

MARYJO.
AWAY IN A MANGER NO CRIB FOR A BED,
THE LITTLE LORD JESUS LAYS DOWN HIS SWEET
HEAD—

(Now ALL come from their areas into area where G.I. is.)

SISSY. Then we go carolling where all the amputees are—

MARYJO.
THE STARS IN HEAVEN LOOK DOWN WHERE HE
LAY
THE LITTLE LORD JESUS ASLEEP IN THE HAY

MARTHA. (*To Sissy and Leeann.*) There's one boy here who's just had his legs and arm blown off—this morning—just eighteen—

(SHE kneels behind G.I. holding his head. SISSY and LEEANN move close.)

LEEANN. We go very close to him—
MARYJO.
I LOVE YOU LORD JESUS
LOOK DOWN FROM THE SKY—
SISSY. Tears are starting down this guy's face—
G.I. (*To Sissy.*) I have your picture—
SISSY. What?
G.I. Breast pocket—get it out—
SISSY. (*To Leeann.*) It must be *him*! The guy from the Bob Hope Show! (*SHE pulls out the picture from GI's pocket.*)
LEEANN. Of all his worldly possessions!
SISSY. *My* picture! Wants *me* to have it! *Knows* he's dying—(*To G.I.*) Oh, soldier, you'll be okay! I promise you, you'll be fine—
G.I. (*Softly.*) Take it—remember me—
SISSY. Now how could I ever forget a handsome guy like you?
MARYJO.
AND STAY BY MY CRADLE—

(SISSY runs from area, MARYJO stops singing.)

SISSY. (*To audience.*) I can't! I can't! I can't!

(WHITNEY blows out the candle and moves into new area.)

WHITNEY. *(To audience.)* It wasn't just the soldiers that tore us apart—
MARYJO. *(Moving to new area too.)* But the Vietnamese too—
WHITNEY. *(To audience.)* 'Cause they were smart—funny—hardworking—
MARYJO. *(To audience.)* And we were fighting on their land—
WHITNEY. *(To audience.)* They'd come to work at The Red Cross Center early mornings—

(Vietnamese MUSIC is heard.
LEEANN enters area as BIEN, moving to music. SHE wears a head scarf. SHE holds clave sticks which she hits together.)

MARYJO. *(To audience.)* Smiling—whistling—singing while they cleaned—
WHITNEY. *(To audience.)* My housekeeper Bien works at The Red Cross Center too—

(SHE looks at LEEANN [BIEN]. LEEANN [BIEN] hits clave sticks again, kneels scrubbing floor.)

WHITNEY. Oh, good morning Bien—
LEEANN. *(As BIEN.)* Good morning Miss Whitney. What I do this morning please? File paper? Run errand headquarter please?

WHITNEY. (*To audience.*) In the afternoon when we leave the Center, Bien takes me to market. And I show *her* American cooking—(*To Bien.*) Then you pour the milk gravy over the meat, Bien, and serve with sauerkraut. It's sauerbraten.

LEEANN. (*As BIEN. Pronouncing word with difficulty.*) Sauerbraten?

WHITNEY. Here. Taste.

LEEANN. (*As BIEN.*) Oh Miss Whitney—you eat this? Oh no Miss Whitney! Oh no!

(SHE hits clave sticks together, then points with one to Martha, almost as if it were a baton or a remote control.)

MARTHA. (*To audience.*) On the wards I watch the Vietnamese parents come in. And they lie down and curl right up on the beds. Cuddling their injured kids—

(LEEANN [BIEN] hits sticks together, then points with one to Maryjo.)

MARYJO. (*From her area.*) Then Bien brings Peanut to the Center—cutest little Vietnamese boy! (*To BIEN.*) He's adorable, Bien! And know what? He loves American music. I'm gonna teach him to play my guitar!

LEEANN. (*As BIEN.*) Oh you very nice American lady to Peanut. To all Vietnamese—

(SHE smiles, hits clave sticks together, then points with one to Sissy who is in another area.)

SISSY. (*To audience.*) On the ward *I* treat a mother who's pregnant with another child at home. She's taken a rocket in her face. Cross-section of her face is gone! And she doesn't even whimper in her bed—

(*BIEN hits clave sticks, points with one to Whitney.*)

WHITNEY. (*To audience.*) But I am starting to be troubled by the Vietnamese guards outside our villa at night.

(*BIEN now starts hitting sticks together softly, ominously.*)

LEEANN. (*As BIEN.*) Oh Miss Whitney—guards beat up Cho and Lu— (*SHE continues beating clave sticks, more quickly, more ominously.*)
WHITNEY. Our maids?
LEEANN. (*As BIEN.*) Guards beat up Cho and Lu good!
WHITNEY. But the guards are our friends—aren't they?

(*BIEN beats sticks louder.*)

LEEANN. (*As BIEN.*) Oh they not friend Miss Whitney. They not friend—

(*BIEN points to Sissy with one stick.*)

SISSY. (*To audience.*) Then one night the pregnant mother does whimper—little tears are in her eyes. And I see she's miscarried beneath the sheet. Then they bring her other child to her, her little boy. But he doesn't know her with her bandaged face. And they take her little boy away.

(BIEN hits claves together, then points to Whitney with stick.)

WHITNEY. *(To audience.)* Then the guards come right into my room one night. Steal my stuff right out the door while I watch secretly in bed—
LEEANN. *(As BIEN.)* Oh Miss Whitney they got guns! You watch out Miss Whitney! You watch out.

(BIEN hits sticks, points with one to Martha.)

MARTHA. *(To audience.)* I bring dinner to a POW woman and walk around to help her eat, when she tries to plunge a fork in my back. I whirl around and knock it from her hand.

(BIEN hits sticks, points with one to Whitney.)

WHITNEY. *(To audience.)* Then the guards come back again. Bien's cousin Nguyen who works for us is with them! Emptying my desk—taking documents—holding a gun—Bien? Your *cousin*? I have to report this—

(BIEN, stick beating sticks together, more and more ominously.)

LEEANN. (*As BIEN.*) Oh Nguyen no cousin Bien! You big mistake! Nguyen no cousin Bien! No report nothing! You understand?

(BIEN hits sticks, points to Martha.)

MARTHA. Then she grabs the *knife*, and tries to plunge it in my arm! I knock that from her hand! I injure her!

(BIEN hits sticks, points to Maryjo.)

MARYJO. I can't find Peanut! I want to teach him to sing "Proud Mary." (*To Bien.*) Hey—where's Peanut gone?
LEEANN. (*As BIEN.*) Oh—he dead Miss Maryjo.
MARYJO. What?
LEEANN. (*As BIEN.*) Find him by airfield. American soldier shoot Peanut! Bang! He dead!
MARYJO. They shot Peanut?
LEEANN. (*As BIEN.*) Oh, he VC!
MARYJO. He's eight years old!
LEEANN. (*As BIEN.*) Oh you no trust Peanut! He VC! All his friend, his family VC! (*SHE smiles.*) You want *Bien* sing song with you today?

(SHE hits the sticks, points to Sissy.
SISSY begins to move to new area.)

SISSY. (*To audience.*) And then one night in triage— five G.I.s are carried in. All shot down—(*SHE looks around.*) Hey—we need help in triage—anybody free?

(LEEANN hears, puts sticks in pocket, moving from her area where she was portraying BIEN into SISSY's area for new scene.)

LEEANN. *(To audience.)* And I'm a circulating nurse and I go into triage that night to help—*(SHE goes to Martha and Sissy.)*

MARTHA. *(To audience.)* And we are all working like crazy—

SISSY. *(To audience.)* But we lose all five G.I.s.

LEEANN. *(To audience.)* And I am left with them alone—all the corpses stacked up like cordwood in a little tiny room with me—and then—the door bursts open—and in comes a stretcher with the POW that shot the five G.I.s—

(MARTHA moves toward her.)

LEEANN. And I look at him—and he looks like my sister's son—

MARTHA. *(To Leeann.)* Kid of fifteen! Badly hurt! Take care of him nurse—

LEEANN. *He* killed these five G.I.s? Him?

MARTHA. Take care of him. He's badly hurt—

LEEANN. I—I can't—I can't touch him—*him*?

MARTHA. Nurse!

LEEANN. Get someone else—

MARTHA. There's no one else!

LEEANN. He's—*he's* a Gook?—Gook?—I can't—

MARTHA. Direct order nurse!

LEEANN. No! I'm not here to take care of any gook! You hear me? I can't take care of any gook!

MARTHA. You do what you're told!

LEEANN. Then I'll kill him! KILL HIM! KILL HIM! (*And SHE dives onto floor, pulling clave sticks from pocket and hitting them together very hard, very quick beats as if killing boy, as:*)

SISSY. And she goes for his throat! Hands around his throat!

(SISSY and MARTHA grab Leeann.)

SISSY. Oh God—I've been raised to be a loving person—

LEEANN. (*Slowly sitting up.*) Love my brother as myself—

MARTHA. (*Looking at Leeann.*) I took a vow to help all mankind—

LEEANN. (*Looking at her hands, still holding sticks.*) Regardless of color, race or skin—(*SHE now drops sticks.*)

MARTHA. (*To audience.*) For a long time her hands are shaking—

LEEANN. (*To audience.*) They've been in a death choke around a young boy's throat—who looks like my sister's son!—

SISSY. (*Looking up.*) We are defiling something—something holy is being transgressed here—Jesus? Can you hear?

LEEANN. (*To audience.*) Murder is in my ken—

(STEELE moves into new area carrying report. OTHERS gather in background, listening.)

STEELE. *(To audience.)* "50,000 Chinese"! That's what I titled my report. The one I wrote about the Tet offensive. Because I called it. Thirty days before. And it said we had better get our act together because *this* is what is facing us, *this* is what is going to happen, and it's going to happen on Tet—their New Year. Then I ran right in to the J-2 with my report, excited as all get out. And the Intelligence Officer says:

OFFICER. *(Comes to her.)* Yes, can I help you?

STEELE. Look, we need to disseminate this fast! It's got to be told and acted on!

OFFICER. Take it on up to Saigon. Headquarters. MACV. Tell 'em, up there to send *their* J-2 out.

STEELE. *(To audience.)* So I get in my jeep— *(SHE crosses stage.)* And I go on up to Saigon. *(SHE walks over to Sergeant, salutes.)*

SERGEANT. Yes, can I help you?

STEELE. I'd like to see the J-2 because I've got some information here in this report and we need to disseminate it fast! It's got to be told and acted on.

SERGEANT. Just a minute please, and I'll send the captain out! *(HE turns, about face. Salutes Steele.)*

CAPTAIN. Yes, can I help you?

STEELE. I'd like to see the J-2 because I've got some information here in this report and we need to disseminate it fast! It's got to be told and acted on!

CAPTAIN. I'll send the major out. *(HE about faces and salutes as MAJOR.)*

MAJOR. Yes, can I help you?

STEELE. Yes, sir. I've got some information here in this report, and we need to disseminate it fast! It's got to be told and acted on!

MAJOR. I'll send the colonel out. *(Gives Steele back report. HE about faces and salutes as COLONEL.)*

COLONEL. Yes, can I help you?

STEELE. Yes, sir. We need to disseminate this fast. It's got to be told and acted on!

COLONEL. You don't say—

(STEELE gives it. COLONEL marches away, stands back to Steele other side of stage, reads.)

COLONEL. Hemmm—haww—hem—haw—

STEELE. *(To audience.)* Now the colonel gives it to the major and the major gives it to the captain and the captain gives it to the sergeant and then they start to huddle. And then they go into a room. And then they shut the door. And my, my, they are gone a long time. And then they all come back.

(OFFICER marches back with report.)

ALL THE OFFICERS. Well, *we* don't know—*we* don't think we really better—*we* think "no"—no, no—*we* guess *not*! No! Sorry. But it is definitely a "no"! *(HE gives Steele report, salutes.)*

STEELE. *(Staggered.)* NO??

OFFICER. No! *(OFFICER salutes again, exits.)*

STEELE. *(To audience.)* And I walk out of that office and sit down in my jeep, and first time in nineteen years in the Army, I *cry*! They knew I had the truth! Why wouldn't they listen? Because I called the enemy by an unacceptable *name* in the damn report? "50,000 Chinese"? instead of "50,000 *Vietnamese*"? Or "50,000 *Vietcong*"? Is that what was wrong at Headquarters? Calling it like it is? They *are* Chinese. Or have *I* got the wrong names? Enlisted Specialist instead of Lieutenant? Woman instead of Man? Black instead of White? Black Woman Specialist announcing that The Chinese are going to clobber the bejesus out of us in thirty days? Well, Tet happened—on the nose—turning point of the war—and Tet is history—hundreds—thousands—lost—wasted lives—

(SHE moves away, looks back, watching the following scene. Sound like FIRECRACKERS begins.)

MARTHA. (*Coming forward to the audience.*) First—when Tet began—we thought it was firecrackers because it's their New Year—

LEEANN. (*Coming forward to audience.*) Then the call came—

(MARYJO picks up hand mike. Stands on high platform.)

MARYJO. *(On loudspeaker.)* All staff! Report to hospital at once! Mass casualty coming in! All staff! Report to positions immediately! Mass casualty coming in! All staff! (*SHE keeps repeating under dialogue.*)

SISSY. (*Crawling under a bench as SHE speaks.*) It's a long crawl from your hooch to the Operating Room. But none of us were going to stand up that night!

(LEEANN and MARTHA follow her, crawling under bench.)

LEEANN. Monday night. Two a.m. Running, crawling, slithering along—here in Vietnam—

(LEEANN, MARTHA, SISSY in same area. WHITNEY [NURSE] also in area.)

SISSY. *(To audience.)* Patients start coming in one after the other after the other—I've never seen so many patients in my life!

MARTHA. *(To audience.)* Here's a yellow sheet of paper. Make a list. Worst ones at the top—

LEEANN. *(To audience.)* But they're coming so fast, so fast—

SISSY. *(To audience.)* I keep scratching out names—

MARTHA. *(To audience.)* Start using numbers instead—

SISSY. *(To audience.)* Numbers dancing down the page—

LEEANN. *(To audience.)* Then someone worse comes in—

MARTHA. And I put his number at the top—

(SISSY and LEEANN carry bench, as if it were a stretcher.)

LEEANN. Helter-skelter—
SISSY. Cockeyed numbers dancing down the page—

LEEANN. We put a patient in a room—

MARTHA. And bring another on the floor up close outside the door—

(MARTHA and WHITNEY carry bench to platform.)

SISSY. Waiting—waiting for that room—

MARTHA. Working 'round and 'round the clock— *(Hurries across to bench where patient is.)*

LEEANN. No time to eat.

SISSY. Just grabbing bread and stuffing it down with cokes—*(SISSY carries bench to another platform.)*

MARTHA. Numbers dancing—helter-skelter down that page—

(THEY are all scurrying now.)

LEEANN. A doctor pops benzedrines in our mouths— Checking off our names—moving on—

SISSY. Four hours and he's back. More bennies popping in our mouths.

MARTHA. More names checked off—helter-skelter down the page—

MARYJO. *(On mike.) Attention!* Sapper attack! The *enemy* is penetrating our perimeter. Attention! Be alert! *Sapper attack now in progress from North Quarter of Air Base!* Sapper Attack! Be Alert! *(SHE keeps repeating this, more and more softly, under dialogue now.)*

MARTHA. The *enemy* is coming in *here*? Oh my God!

LEEANN. For our medications! OH GOD!!

(CORPSMAN enters.)

MARTHA. Corpsman! Lock the door! Get your gun and guard the door! QUICK!

CORPSMAN. I can't! Conscientious Objector, Captain! I can't!

MARTHA. Do it! Quick!

CORPSMAN. I can't, Captain! I CAN'T!

MARTHA. DIRECT ORDER! COWARD! DO IT I SAID!!

CORPSMAN. *You'll* have to do it ma'am!

MARTHA. I don't know how to shoot the God damn thing! Get that patient out of bed! Move! Give *him* the rifle!

(EXPLOSION. SCREAMS. MARYJO stops announcement. EVERYONE falls to the floor.)

MARTHA. THE WARD IS HIT!

CORPSMAN. I'M HIT!! *(HE falls.)*

MARTHA. Shrapnel flying through his head! And he falls on me! DEAD!!

(BLACKOUT.)

SISSY. The lights are out!

LEEANN. Open the flashlights!

(FLASHLIGHTS come on, flashing around.)

MARTHA. Chunks of flesh—blood—all over the walls—

LEEANN. Screaming—yelling—smell of burning flesh—

MARTHA. My patients!

LEEANN. Wounded! Again!

SISSY. *Killed*! In their hospital beds!

(MARTHA takes a step forward. CORPSMAN exits.)

MARTHA. *(To audience as SHE moves down from platform to floor level.)* I'm heading into the operating room the fourth day? The fifth? And the tile floor here slopes. And I see water coming out of the scrub sinks splashing on the floor—and patients lying on the floor with blood coming out of them—and then I see the water mixing with the blood and running down the hall—a river! Tet! Nightmare River of Blood! I run out! Oh God! Help me stay behind my wall! God in heaven help me just to walk along!

LEEANN. *(To audience. SHE moves down to floor level.)* Except it's an eighteen-year-old coming into surgery—and he's so young he doesn't even have hair on his face—and I'm running along beside his stretcher, and he's crying—Mommy? Mommy? Mommy? And I'm saying: I'm here, baby—Mommy's right here! Only I'm just twenty-one myself!

(STEELE and WHITNEY joining group.)

SISSY. *(To audience, joining group.)* And he's a blond kid from California looking just like your brother Denny and screaming: I DON'T WANT TO DIE!

MARTHA. (*To audience.*) A piece of my heart goes with each of them! A PIECE OF MY HEART!

(THEY stand, staggered positions in group. A pause, then WHITNEY comes forward.)

WHITNEY. (*To audience.*) A hundred days before you leave you start filling in the short timer's calendar—marking off each day—

STEELE. (*Comes forward. To audience.*) In Saigon the supervisor shows me my name on an enemy "wanted list." I'm number two! Then one day later I'm walking to work when out of nowhere two motorbikes whiz by, knock me down, grab my briefcase and disappear. Next day it happens again. And I belly flop. (*SHE falls to ground, in pain.*) And hurt my back. Bad! And all of a sudden I'm pulling out my .45—And I start shooting wild! (*SHE pulls a gun out.*) I'm gonna blow somebody's head off here! You hear me? I'm gonna blow somebody's head right off here! (*A pause. SHE looks around, stands, starting to come back to her senses.*) Oh God! I have got to go home! I have *got* to go home!

(A pause.)

SISSY. (*To audience.*) Getting a little crazy now—thinking about getting out—

MARTHA. (*To audience.*) Wanting to go—not wanting to go—

MARYJO. Best year of my life—worst year of my life—

STEELE. Such a sisterhood, brotherhood, comradeship. Like no other place—no other time on earth—

WHITNEY. (*To others.*) DEROS day! I don't care how I get out of here! But somebody just get me out! If I smell another piece of dried fish on a wall or pour another glass of Kool-Aid, I am going to start screaming and never stop! (*SHE heads up towards airplane platform.*)

LEEANN. (*Looking in diary.*) Wednesday. The 12th. I walk into the hospital to say goodbye. Strangely quiet day. Everybody's standing around. Suddenly the double doors burst open and two litter bearers run in, set down their litter, run out. And I look and see a little Vietnamese boy and girl—both with their hands chopped off. Looking at us. All of us gaping, dumb, numb—I walk out the door of the hospital in silence—for the last time—here in Vietnam.

(*LEEANN moves to airplane platform where OTHERS are gathered.*
G.I. enters. SISSY is getting on airplane platform.)

SISSY. (*To audience.*) Patient follows me onto the airstrip. Watches me climb the stairs to my plane. (*To G.I.*) Take care, soldier—(*SHE gives him a bright smile.*)

G.I. Hey, you've got the biggest damn smile in all of Nam!

SISSY. Because this plane's *my* Freedom Bird! I am going home!

G.I. Good luck—

(All WOMEN now on high platform [airplane]. SISSY waves at soldier. HE waves back from ground level, then salutes.)

BLACKOUT

END OF ACT I

ACT II

LIGHTS UP. The WOMEN sit on benches on high platform, airplane.

WHITNEY. (*As AIRLINE ATTENDANT. On mike.*) Attention! All passengers, please! Attention! The captain is beginning our descent. Attention all passengers, please! Attention!

(THEY begin to look out window.)

MARYJO. Oh my God! Look! McDonald's golden arches! Down there! Look! I can't wait.

LEEANN. The Space Needle! Look!

MARTHA. The Golden Gate Bridge? Yes! It is! Look— look down there!

SISSY. The skyline—look—over there—LOOK!

(More CHEERS, WHISTLES, APPLAUSE. WOMEN stand up.)

WHITNEY. (*As ATTENDANT. On mike.*) We have just landed!

EVERYONE. (*Ad-libbing.*) We're home! That's *it!* Oh, my God, we're here! We made it! LOOK!

WHITNEY. (*As ATTENDANT. On mike.*) Attention all passengers! Please remain in your seats with seatbelts securely fastened until the aircraft has come to a complete stop!

(THEY jump up, climb off airplane platform.)

    SISSY. The doors open and we rush to push out—
    LEEANN. Run out—
    MARTHA. And down the stairs and—
    WHITNEY. Kneel on the ground—*(SHE kneels.)*
    MARYJO. Fall on the ground—*(SHE falls.)*
    STEELE. And kiss the ground!

(THEY all kiss ground.)

    EVERYONE. *American soil*!

(THEY now rise, SISSY and STEELE moving to one area, MARTHA, WHITNEY to other areas.)

    SISSY. *(To audience.)* I go to Ft. Lewis to get processed out.
    MARTHA. *(To audience.)* I go to Oakland.
    WHITNEY. *(To audience.)* I go to McCord—

(Sound of CLAVES, beating as THEY all scurry. THEY stop as CLAVES stop.)

    STEELE. *(As OFFICER. To Sissy.)* ... but it's too late, Captain, to process you now. Sorry! Have to wait for morning for that.
    SISSY. I can't wait for morning. I'm going home!

STEELE. (*As OFFICER.*) I'm really sorry, Captain—

(*SISSY turns away.*)

STEELE. Wait! *I'll* process you! Take you on over to SeaTac Airport for your next flight. Come on!

SISSY. (*Starts across stage. To audience.*) And she does.

(*SISSY stops at Martha in new area of stage.*)

SISSY. (*To Martha.*) Next flight to San Francisco, please!

MARTHA. (*As AGENT.*) That's tomorrow morning, ma'am.

SISSY. I can't wait that long! I'm—

MARTHA. (*As AGENT.*) Just back from Vietnam?

SISSY. Yes! And I'm trying to—

MARTHA. (*As AGENT.*) Get home?

SISSY. Yes!

MARTHA. (*As AGENT.*) Follow me—there's another airline—I'll get you on!

SISSY. (*To audience.*) And she does!

(*Sound of CLAVES beating, as LEEANN comes forward, THEY stop.*)

LEEANN. (*To audience.*) I'm in my boonie hat, Vietnam posters in one hand, shopping bags full of ticking clocks in the other! From my stopover in Japan! And how am I gonna get to SeaTac Airport for my next plane?

Nobody is telling me where to go and I can't find my group and my family isn't allowed to meet me here!

(FATHER enters, comes to Leeann.)

FATHER. Nurse—nurse? Want a lift to SeaTac, nurse?
LEEANN. Taxi driver?
FATHER. Gold Star Father! Lost my only son in Vietnam—
LEEANN. Oh I'm sorry—I'm sorry—
FATHER. Know what I do? Keep track of when these flights come in—meet everybody I can—drive 'em on over to get their next plane—come on!

(And FATHER starts hurrying across stage, LEEANN behind him.)

LEEANN. (*To audience.*) And he piles the clocks in, *and* my gear in, *and* me in my boonie hat—and away we go!

(Sound of CLAVES beating, as FATHER exits. WHITNEY, MARTHA come forward in another area.)

WHITNEY. (*To audience.*) It's time for Jane's departure ... we've served together the whole year ... (*To Martha [NEW NURSE].*) I am dreading leaving you—
MARTHA. (*As NEW NURSE.*) Well, I can't picture life without you—
WHITNEY. You were always there for me, you know?
MARTHA. (*As NEW NURSE.*) I know—

(Sound of CLAVES beating.)

LEEANN. *(From her area of stage, to audience.)* When I get off my plane in San Francisco, a G.I. heroin addict tumbles down the stairs onto the tarmac and hits his head. Hard! I run to him, kneeling, blood pouring from him to my uniform. The ambulance takes him off and I hurry to the counter for my next plane.

(SHE turns to AGENT who's come to her area.)

AGENT. Sorry, lady, but you can't get on the plane like *that!*

LEEANN. Like what?

AGENT. Like bloody from head to foot!

LEEANN. I helped a soldier! I just got back from The Nam.

AGENT. I don't care if you just got back from the moon! You're not getting on *our* plane like that!

LEEANN. *(To audience.)* And he kicks my suitcase! Off the scale! Breaking the lock! My stuff spilling all over the airport floor!

(Sound of CLAVES beating as AGENT exits, SISSY comes forward.)

SISSY. *(To audience.)* I fly to Erie, Pennsylvania, drive up my street to my big white house—*(SHE runs up stairs to a platform.)* And I see lighted torches all the way across my yard! And a huge banner saying:

(MARTHA coming into area OTHERS behind her forming group.)

MARTHA. *(As MOM.)* Hello Sissy!

SISSY. *(To Martha, embracing her.)* Oh Mom!

MARTHA. *(As MOM.)* And there's Dad—And Denny—and Joe—Aunt Ellen—Uncle Ben—and Cousin Sue—

SISSY. And Grandmother? Where is she?

MARTHA. *(As MOM.)* Waiting—in her bedroom—

SISSY. *(Turns to Steele on ramp.)* Grandmother!

STEELE. *(As GRANDMOTHER.)* Thank you Jesus! For bringing my Sister home!

(Sound of CLAVES beating as MARTHA steps forward.)

MARTHA. *(To audience.)* When I go home my father says—

FATHER. *(Enters.)* Well Martha—You've done us proud! Fought the good fight.

MARTHA. Yes, sir! Did my best, sir.

FATHER. Staying in I suppose? You know, twenty years and the benefits are outstanding! Outstanding! *(FATHER exiting as:)*

MARTHA. *(Profoundly hurt.)* Not sure, sir ... about staying in ... sir ... *(SHE looks away.)*

(Sound of CLAVES beating as WHITNEY comes forward.)

WHITNEY. *(To audience.)* I check into the Red Cross Center—and they strip me of *all* my military ID—my

card—my government papers—and what they don't take—
they *change*! Inkout! Blot out! Cut out!

*(SHE looks frightened, stunned, sound of CLAVES
beating as STEELE comes towards a platform with a
bench.)*

STEELE. *(To audience.)* I go home on furlough to
Mississippi. And that evening my whole family sits down
to watch the news—

*(STEELE and EVERYONE sits. MALE TV
ANNOUNCER enters, addresses them.)*

MALE TV ANNOUNCER. *(To others.)* ... and now the
report today on casualties in Vietnam.
STEELE. *(To audience.)* And it's all a pack of lies.
MALE TV ANNOUNCER. We had twenty casualties
reported—
STEELE. *(To audience.)* It's double that!
MALE TV ANNOUNCER. —as opposed to thirty
yesterday.
STEELE. *(To audience.) Triple* that!
MALE TV ANNOUNCER. So the count is down for
today.
STEELE. *(To audience.)* Any *fool* knows that!
MALE TV ANNOUNCER. That makes a total of fifty
men lost so far this week. North Vietnam casualties
reported at fifteen hundred so far this week ... And now for
the local news. On the north side ...

LEEANN. (*As NIECE.*) Huh! That's not so bad is it? Right, Aunt Steeley? Fifty to fifteen hundred's not so bad at all!

STEELE. (*To audience.*) They are talking about *people*! It's not a baseball score! Somewhere in that statistical body count are young boys who died! Souls got lost in there. But how can I tell them that?

(TV ANNOUNCER leaves, sound of CLAVES beating as MARYJO moves into new area.)

MARYJO. (*To audience.*) A friend takes me shopping for underwear. Sears Roebuck in the mall.

(SISSY comes into area.)

SISSY. (*As FRIEND.*) There, Maryjo—Sears is down there—South end—

MARYJO. (*To audience.*) The Mall is gigantic! People in front of me, beside me, behind me. Shopping! Wearing green! Oh God I can't stand GREEN! Driving me nuts! KHAKI GREEN!

SISSY. (*As FRIEND.*) I want to price some shoes in that boutique—go on and get your stuff—I'll meet you in Sears at the checkout, okay? (*SISSY walks away.*)

MARYJO. (*To audience.*) I get the underwear, go to the counter—money in one hand, pants, bras in the other—and the clerk at the register is looking at me, smiling at me,— WEARING KHAKI GREEN! Oh my God! I don't belong here! I DON'T BELONG HERE AT ALL! (*SHE runs across stage.*) And I run out. Money, pants and bras—

SISSY. (*As FRIEND.*) Maryjo! Stop! Come back! What's wrong with you?

MARYJO. Nothing! I—I got lost—I—

(*Sound of CLAVES beating as LEEANN comes into new area, as ALL except MARTHA form protestors line.*)

LEEANN. (*To audience.*) I end up on a bus down to L.A. to see my friend. In the depot I see people waving signs—

(*PROTESTORS start marching. Heavy steps. In line. Up and down steps and platforms. THEY march past Leeann, yelling in her face.*)

OTHERS. (*As PROTESTORS. To Leeann.*) PEACE NOW! PEACE NOW! HEY HEY LBJ, HOW MANY KIDS DID YOU KILL TODAY? MAKE LOVE, NOT WAR! PEACE NOW! (*THEY move away circling stage.*)

LEEANN. (*As MARTHA comes into area.*) My friend comes running up—

MARTHA. (*As FRIEND.*) What's all that blood stain? Jesus! You got a dress in your bag?

LEEANN. What?

MARTHA. (*As FRIEND.*) Dress, jeans—civvies—something else to wear?

LEEANN. It's my uniform! It's got all my medals on!

MARTHA. (*As FRIEND.*) Go in the ladies room and change!

LEEANN. No!

MARTHA. (*As FRIEND.*) You're a target!

LEEANN. Target?

(The PROTESTORS are back again, yelling right in her face, spitting.)

OTHERS. (*As PROTESTORS.*) MURDERER! PIG! BUTCHER! BLOODY KILLER! GO BACK TO NAM! WAR MONGER! GET OUT OF HERE! BLOODY SCUM!

(THEY move upstage, stop, watch.)

MARTHA. (*As FRIEND.*) Change, will you? For God's sake! They throw stones, tomatoes—they'll spit.

LEEANN. (*To audience.*) So I run to the washroom, change out of my uniform, I run back. (*To Martha.*) Burn it! (*SHE throws duffle on ground.*)

MARTHA. (*As FRIEND.*) But your medals—here— take your medals off at least—

LEEANN. FUCK MY MEDALS! BURN IT, I SAID!!

(Sound of CLAVES beating, as WHITNEY enters new area, sitting on bench.)

WHITNEY. (*To audience.*) I stay overnight in a Seattle hotel and in the evening I go into the cocktail lounge. The Nam's a figment of my imagination now. My memories are all I have—(*SHE starts to drink. MAN enters.*) Then a man comes in—

MAN. Hi! You attending the pharmaceutical convention? Thought I saw you up at the third floor display—(*HE sits by her.*)

WHITNEY. No—I—I just got back from The Nam—

MAN. Hey—you kiddin' me? Nice girl like you in a war like that? (*HE laughs, subtly.*)

WHITNEY. (*Indignant.*) I was with The American Red Cross!

MAN. Son of a bitch! Classy girl like you a Doughnut Dolly? "Pourin' Kool Aid?" (*HE chuckles.*)

WHITNEY. (*To audience.*) I can't stand him!

MAN. God, sure a screwed up policy we're pursuing over there, huh?

WHITNEY. I don't know about that!

MAN. Aw, now don't get sore—here—buy you a drink?

WHITNEY. No. Thank you. I prefer to drink alone!

MAN. Look—it's not your fault about the war, okay? I mean *everything* about it is *so* screwed up that—

WHITNEY. (*Interrupting.*) The boys are not screwed up! The poor grunts in the field are just obeying orders! They are fighting a war!

MAN. Must be what they want to do, though.

WHITNEY. What?

MAN. I mean, they didn't have to go in the first place, right?

WHITNEY. (*To audience.*) I can't be around him another minute! (*SHE rises.*)

MAN. Million easy ways to avoid the draft—

WHITNEY. (*To audience.*) I have got to get away from him!

(*And SHE runs from area, MAN calling after her.*)

MAN. Hey—come back! (*HE now looks at all of the women.*) What's wrong with you?

MARTHA. (*From her area. To audience.*) Is something wrong with me?

WHITNEY. (*To audience.*) I don't fit in with people like him anymore.

STEELE. (*To audience.*) Or my family.

MARYJO. (*To audience.*) Or my old friends.

MARTHA. They all have feelings I don't understand.

LEEANN. I have feelings I don't understand.

SISSY. I thought everything would be different when I got back.

WHITNEY. I am the only thing that's different since I got back—

STEELE. (*Comes into new area. To audience.*) Well, I am feelin' proud. New Warrant Officer—WO-1! Three rows of good stuff on this side of my chest—couple of pretty little ribbons on this other side to match! Not bad! I'm back here at Ft. Bragg, walkin' on into the colonel's office to see what new and exciting assignment I'm going to get because of these three tough years in Nam!

(*SHE walks to area where COLONEL appears. THEY salute.*)

COLONEL. Hello Officer Steele, hello!

STEELE. Hello, Colonel! Hello! (*STEELE salutes again.*)

COLONEL. Well, I've got your wonderful assignment Officer Steele. Wonderful!

STEELE. Well, wonderful, Colonel! Wonderful!

COLONEL. Just the ticket for you—(*HE beams.*) Gonna put you in CONTIC, Steele!

STEELE. I beg your pardon, sir?

COLONEL. CONTIC Steele. Perfect placement for you at this time!

STEELE. But that's exactly the job I started out in sir—here—before I went to Nam!

COLONEL. Perfect, isn't it? Just what the doctor ordered all right!

STEELE. Oh now, just a minute, sir—

COLONEL. Some problem for you Officer Steele?

STEELE. Well, sir, I did three years in The Nam, sir. And that was three years of hell. Now you are telling me I'm supposed to come back here and take back my old job here at Ft. Bragg? Well, now sir, ending up where you were three years before seems to me a me a further sentence in hell. And I feel I'm entitled to a little heaven, sir!

COLONEL. But it's an easy desk job Steele—and with that back injury—report says you're in a brace—probable surgery down the road—

STEELE. I'm in Intelligence sir! Workin' with my brain, sir—not my—back!

COLONEL. Well—still and all Steele—still and all—

STEELE. All *what*? Sir?

(COLONEL walks away. STEELE turns to audience.)

STEELE. Still—and all—what?

MARYJO. (*Steps in new area. To audience.*) We go to our agent in L.A. The Sugar Candies and I. To get our salaries for our year's work—

*(SISSY, MARTHA, LEEANN, STEELE as BACK-UPS
sit close by as AGENT enters area coming to Maryjo.)*

AGENT. Look girls—I'm sorry about this—but
there've been operating cost problems—unforeseeable. Just
about manage to reimburse the airfares I'm afraid—

MARYJO. *(Stunned.)* *Airfares*? You owe us $1,000 a
month a piece! That's what's coming to us!

AGENT. Sorry girls. Best I can do.

MARYJO. *You* got paid! There were government
contracts for every gig we played. A lot of money changed
hands!

AGENT. Look—you want the refund on the tickets or
what?

MARYJO. A whole year risking our lives for the
airfare? Are you kidding or what? We could sue you,
mister.

AGENT. *(Chuckling.)* *Sue me*? You have no written
agreements. Now let's move it, girls. I've got an act
auditioning in here. Let's move it out!

(HE walks HER out.)

MARYJO. *(To audience.)* We go up and down the coast
looking for gigs. No one will hire us—we go back to the
Agent. *(SHE turns back to him. To Agent.)* Help us get a
job—please?—

AGENT. *(To Maryjo.)* Too much anger in your voice—
tension through your whole body! Clientele in night clubs
like sweet sounds. Soft, sexy girls. Next? *(HE moves
away.)*

MARYJO. (*To audience.*) We split up.

(*BACK-UPS move away.*)

MARYJO. (*To audience.*) I sleep all day. Stop singing. Stop playing the guitar. Shove it back of my closet. Cannot *stand* the sight of that guitar!

(*SHE shoves guitar in case under bench. CLAVES beat as LEEANN comes forward.*)

LEEANN. (*To audience.*) I'm sent to Fitzsimmons. Fourteen months to serve. Lower extremity orthopedic ward. Ninety percent amputees from Nam. Paraplegics, quadriplegics. Whee! It's going to be like Nam. It's not— the G.I.s are different to me—used to be grateful—now nothing's good enough for them! And I am giving the best care in the world! I am a super nurse by now, right? I am just about walking on water for these guys and what *more* is it these guys are wanting from me?

MARTHA. (*Moves to Leeann's area. To audience.*) I leave the service. I'm civilian now. Texas Medical Center. Dr. Cooley—the heart surgeon. God, it feels exciting here—like Nam. It's not—(*To Leeann.*)There is nothing here but competition. Nurses to nurses and nurses to doctors and doctors to doctors. Cardiac arrest comes in and everybody *fighting* to get in on it. I can't believe it—you know?

LEEANN. In Nam whoever was good at it did it!

MARTHA. We had a sergeant there good at heart massage and we'd all get *out* of his way to let *him* work.

LEEANN. I was treated different in Nam. Didn't have to compete. Trusted—gut level—

MARTHA. I sensed something wrong, I'd say—I don't know exactly *what* this is—but it's *something*.

LEEANN. And then you and the doctor go to work on the guy.

MARTHA. Here, the doctor says, "Well, nurse, we really haven't got time to check out your 'hunches,' all right?"

LEEANN. (*To audience.*) I'm out of the service. San Francisco. Intensive care. They won't let me hang a pint of blood without supervision by the IV Nurse! I have put in more IVs in my year in Nam than she will do in her lifetime! Who the hell is *she* to evaluate *my* skills?

MARTHA. (*To audience.*) They send me to classes to learn the new EKG Monitor. And I can't learn anything new! I'm losing confidence—I'm getting self-conscious about my nursing skills—(*SHE turns away.*)

LEEANN. (*To Martha.*) Final insult! Ultimate degradation: they are putting me through an Orientation Course about CPR. Oh, I am getting a real "attitude" problem now!

MARTHA. (*Turning back to Leeann.*) I wake up depressed—

LEEANN. I *never* want to go to work—

MARTHA. If I could just figure out why I'm not retaining what I learn—

LEEANN. I quit!

MARTHA. (*To audience.*) I go back into the military. The Reserves. To teach. A chance to show my skills. (*To Leeann.*) I can't stand these Reserve nurses! They played it safe during Nam. Why aren't they active? All these nurses paid for *practicing*? Why don't they go do what they're practicing for *I* quit!

LEEANN. Job to job to job—

MARTHA. Looking—for the respect—the thrill—the challenge—

LEEANN. Four jobs, five jobs, six—

MARTHA. Moving place to place to place—

LEEANN. Homesick for the G.I.s of Nam—

MARTHA. The caring—

LEEANN. The push—

MARTHA. "Adrenalin Junkies" that's us!

LEEANN. Ungodly emergencies and you just got right in there and did the work! CAN DO!

MARTHA. "Nothin' means nothin'" here! It "don't mean a thing"—

LEEANN. Why are we trying to change attitudes over there anyway? What business is it of ours?

MARTHA. Oh, you better put the lid on *that* Pandora's box or you'll go nuts.

LEEANN. (*To audience.*) I stop putting Nam down on my application form. I demonstrate *against* the war! I march! I carry signs!

(*LIGHTS shift to red. Decadent, hellish feeling. A rock torch song from the sixties with female vocal begins and continues under until MUSIC OUT cue as indicated. MARYJO climbs on bench on high platform, beer bottle in hand.*)

MARYJO. (*Drinking beer now, moving to music. To audience.*) I start hitting the bars—hanging out—

drinking—looking for Vets—I'm still attractive—I can go into a bar and there are always men who'll talk to me—

(OTHER WOMEN now group around in background, as if in disco bar, moving subtly to music. ONE might stand on a bench, ONE or TWO also drinking beer, as WHITNEY, drink in hand, moves downstage center, sitting on bench swaying to music.)

MARYJO. *(To audience.)* One night a Vet comes in and we start talking and I feel a connection to this guy—Clint! And he takes me to a party—Vietnam Vets Against the War! *(SHE takes a swig from bottle, listens to music for a beat then steps down from bench and starts moving around.)* Everyone's getting high—standing middle of the room—bouncing up and down—VIBRATING—like Nam!

WHITNEY. *(Looks up at audience.)* I meet Steve at a Vet Center where I'm a social worker. And I think I'm falling in love with Steve—*(SHE drains her glass, pours another from bottle.)* Except he says he doesn't love me. Or anyone. He can't commit to *anything* anymore—he *says!* *(SHE drinks.)* So how can I stay with him when he tells me such things? I can't!

(SHE drinks more, unsteadily lights cigarette, MARYJO has moved downstage near Whitney.)

MARYJO. *(To audience.)* Clint and I start getting very tight and he goes on drunken binges and gets pretty wild— but it doesn't bother me! I get drunk with him—smoke dope—we move in together—*(SHE moves to music.)*

WHITNEY. (*To audience.*) Then I meet Richard at the Great Lakes Naval Hospital where I work in Recreation. And I like Richard very much—a doctor who's been in Nam—except he's not divorced yet—and I don't know if he'll ever go through with it—

MARYJO. (*To audience.*) We go to the mountains in Colorado. Clint and me! Mountain dwellers! In the Cliffs!

WHITNEY. (*To audience.*) Richard breaks off with me—goes back to his wife—

MARYJO. (*To audience.*) Clint and I have this big fight. And he leaves. And I freak out.

WHITNEY. (*To audience.*) Then I meet Pete from Pleiku. But we never really talk about what he's been through. We never really talk about what I've been through. We never really talk about The Nam at all—

MARYJO. (*To audience.*) And I follow Clint cross-country to Vermont and we live together again. And we are having good times and hard times and we are living together for six years—and I think Clint's a good man—

WHITNEY. (*To audience.*) Then Pete decides to go back to Nam. Just like that! And he goes! And why are all these guys deserting me?

MARYJO. (*To audience.*) We start going downhill—and I don't want to split up but Clint wants to split up. And I try to figure out some way to prevent it—but he won't even talk to me—

WHITNEY. (*To audience.*) I don't want to be around men anymore at all! I don't even want to talk to a man! All they do is run out.

MARYJO. (*To audience.*) He is raging, crying, having fits. Gun under his pillow—going for knives—and I am scared to death of him—

WHITNEY. (*To audience.*) Men wanted that war! Made that war! WOMEN NEVER MADE A WAR LIKE *THAT* IN THEIR LIVES!!

MARYJO. (*To audience.*) We split up and I'm in pieces for a year—

(*Sound of MUSIC OUT.*)

WHITNEY. (*To audience.*) *All* my friends are women now—

MARYJO. (*To audience.*) We were never married. But it sure feels like we got divorced.

(*SISSY comes forward to Maryjo [DANIELLE] whom SHE embraces.*)

SISSY. (*To audience.*) When my daughter, Danielle is born, she has an eye defect. Nobody notices it but me. The doctor says it isn't there. So I let it pass. Then she gets bad stomachaches. Then headaches too. I take her for an exam.

(*DANIELLE is behind Sissy, hanging onto Sissy's back, peeking around. OTHERS as doctors on platforms sit looking down at them.*
SISSY with MARYJO [DANIELLE] turns to MARTHA [DOCTOR].)

SISSY. Well, doctor, what do you think?

MARTHA. (*As DOCTOR.*) Can't really put my finger on anything concrete. Not a regular eye problem. Which means it's probably trivial.

SISSY. But the headaches? And the stomachaches? She's so young! This just doesn't seem normal to me at all!

MARTHA. (*As DOCTOR. Smiling.*) Know what? Little knowledge is a dangerous thing! Don't let that old nursing background of yours get in the way!

SISSY. Okay—but run some tests anyhow?

MARTHA. (*As DOCTOR.*) I suppose—

(*SISSY with MARYJO [DANIELLE] turns away.*)

SISSY. (*On phone.*) Hello? You get the results back?

MARTHA. (*Turns around. As DOCTOR, on phone.*) Know what? You were right! Blood work's way off— almost like rheumatic fever. I'm going to call it a "subclinical rheumatic fever." I'll treat her for that, okay?

SISSY. (*On phone.*) Okay ... (*To audience, as SHE crosses stage with DANIELLE in tow.*) Then we move to another town. And I take her to a doctor there ...

(*SHE goes to STEELE [DOCTOR] on another platform.*)

STEELE. (*As DOCTOR.*) Yes, something is wrong. But it's not "*subclinical* rheumatic fever"! That's nonsense!! There's no such thing! Either you have it or you don't. And she doesn't. Let's watch her for a while.

(*SISSY moves away, helps DANIELLE sit.*)

SISSY. (*To audience.*) Six months and I go back—(*To Steele.*) She's breaking out in rashes now—and complaining of pains in her knee joint when she runs—

STEELE. (*As DOCTOR.*) That's growing pains! Bring
her back next year—kids outgrow these things!

(*STEELE turns away. SISSY turns to Danielle.*)

SISSY. Danielle?
MARYJO. (*As DANIELLE.*) What Mommy?
SISSY. Look, Danielle—way over there—far end of the
field—see?
MARYJO. (*As DANIELLE.*) Where?
SISSY. All those colts, sweetheart—running—the little
brown colts—near the barn—
MARYJO. (*As DANIELLE.*) I don't even see the
barn—
SISSY. (*Turns to Doctor.*) Doctor how are the eyes this
year?
STEELE. (*As DOCTOR.*) 20/200 in both eyes!
SISSY. (*Turning back to Danielle.*) They were 20/40
just last year!
STEELE. (*As DOCTOR.*) Mystifying isn't it?
SISSY. (*Turning back to Doctor.*) And two years later?
STEELE. (*As DOCTOR.*) 20/350 left eye, 20/375 right
eye! Amazing situation here!
SISSY. *Do something*! Her stomach hurts all the time!
And she's got headaches every day. What's wrong with her?
MARYJO. (*As DANIELLE.*) Mom? My knee's hurting
again—when I bend! And my feet feel numb, Mom? Make
them operate *again*!

(*SISSY turns to Danielle, then runs over to MARTHA
[DOCTOR].*)

SISSY. Doctor, *I'm* having knee pains too—hiking, biking, climbing stairs—

(SHE now runs to Leeann, Whitney, [DOCTORS] in another area.)

SISSY. Doctor, I'm getting skin rashes too. *(SHE now runs back to Steele [DOCTOR])* Doctor, I had two breast tumors removed. *(SHE now turns to audience.)* Doctor, what is Agent Orange Disease?

(WHITNEY from new area picks up hand mike.)

WHITNEY. *(As VA SPOKESPERSON. To audience front on mike.)* There is no such animal as Agent Orange Disease. Here at the Veterans' Administration we are doing exploratory studies *only*. And obviously there is no medical treatment I can offer you, madam, since the disease simply doesn't exist!

MARYJO. *(As DANIELLE.)* Mom? My other knee is hurting now. I can't bend it to walk. I want *another* operation! Mom?

WHITNEY. *(As SPOKESPERSON. Front on mike.)* We don't handle children, besides, sounds like you've got an inherited, family problem on your hands, madam.

SISSY. *(Front.)* There is no history on either side of the family of anything remotely resembling this! Her father and I both served in Cu Chi! This is Agent Orange Disease!

WHITNEY. *(AS VA SPOKESPERSON. On mike.)* But I've told you madam, there is no such animal as Agent

Orange Disease! (*SHE looks in new direction. On mike.*) Client 3529? This way please—

MARTHA. (*Comes forward. To audience.*) I start teaching nurses for the VA. Clinical Psych class: "The Treatment of Vietnam Vets." Good for me to talk about this—get all that stuff I've got stored behind that wall out into the open at last! First morning I'm so nervous, I'm hanging onto my desk—but it will all work out I think—

SISSY. (*Comes forward. To audience.*) My husband gets a job in Southern California, and we move. Great climate for Danielle—good omen for all of us I think—

WHITNEY. (*Comes forward. To audience.*) I go home to my parents for the holidays. Good to see them after all these years—good to spend Christmas with them I think—

STEELE. (*Comes forward. To audience.*) Well, I finally go for surgery on the back. Good for me to do this I think—but afterwards, they wheel me back—and there's an IV in my arm—and I am pretty groggy—half asleep—when I hear a parade somewhere outside—

(*PARADE MUSIC, distorted, is heard far away. LEEANN comes forward.*)

LEEANN. (*To audience.*) I'm on duty in Emergency. And a fourteen-year-old black boy comes in cut up from a fight. But he won't let me near him. Wants a black nurse. Calls me a "yellow gook bitch!"

WHITNEY. (*To audience.*) Except I can't stop drinking! Even here! At my parents' home! I'm quietly drunk in the corner while they sing carols around the piano Christmas eve—

(Distant sound of CAROLERS added to parade music, distorted.)

SISSY. *(To audience.)* Then five o'clock in the afternoon commercial helicopters start flying over my house. I'm making dinner ... *(Sound of HELICOPTERS [choppers] but a synthesized, DISTORTED sort of sound, is added.)* Stove on—meat frying—I run into the backyard—look up at the commercial planes—they're *NAM* choppers. I'm back in Nam—

MARTHA. *(To audience.)* I look at my lecture notes. The yellow page of numbers from Tet! Numbers dancing! Helter skelter down the yellow page! There! And there! AND THERE!

(SOUND louder.)

WHITNEY. And I look at my family singing—and bandaged G.I.s on the wards at Christmas look back at me!

STEELE. Then they fire off a cannon in that parade outside. *(Sound of CANNON DISTORTED, is added.)* And I jump out of my hospital bed, the IV ripping from my arm. BLOOD? I run out of the ward. I've been hit! Help me! I've been hit!

(Cacophony of SOUNDS still louder.)

SISSY. *(Looking skyward.)* How big a mass casualty on the chopper? How many double amps for me to nurse?

LEEANN. "GOOK!" I scream at the black boy going for his throat. "I didn't come here to take care of any Gook!"

STEELE. Bullet spinning, spinning, ripping to pieces in me! Helicopter swooping down, picking up everybody but me! Hey—don't leave me—I HURT TOO!

(All SOUND out.)

WHITNEY. *(Takes a step. To audience, with difficulty.)* Good evening—my name is Whitney—and I am an alcoholic—but I didn't drink today—or yesterday—or the day before—and I am holding down a job now—*(SHE begins toward a new area, gaining strength as SHE moves.)*

MARTHA. *(Softly, to audience.)* It's getting worse—*(SHE starts toward Whitney's area. SHE carries a bench.)*

STEELE. *(To audience.)* Chills. *(SHE starts toward Whitney's area. SHE carries a bench.)*

LEEANN. *(To audience.)* Night sweats. *(Starting to Whitney.)*

SISSY. *(To audience.)* Shakes. *(Starting to Whitney, carrying a bench.)*

MARYJO. *(To audience.)* Crazy things that nobody would understand. *(Starting to Whitney.)*

LEEANN. *(On phone.)* Hello? I'm calling about the VA Rap group ...

WHITNEY. *(On phone.)* You a Nam vet?

(The WOMEN are now grouping four benches into a square configuration.)

MARTHA. (*On phone.*) Yes. Are the groups vets?

STEELE. (*On phone.*) Women from Nam?

WHITNEY. (*On phone.*) Yes.

MARYJO. (*On phone.*) Because *I'm* not crazy.

MARTHA. *(On phone.)* I can still function okay—

SISSY. (*On phone.*) It's just I have flashes sometimes.

MARTHA. (*On phone.*) And dreams—

LEEANN. (*On phone.*) I called before—about the group therapy sessions?

MARTHA. (*On phone.*) But not *therapy*, right?

WHITNEY. (*On phone.*) It's just a talk group—I sort of moderate—doesn't mean anything is wrong with you at all—

(WOMEN now sit on benches. WHITNEY stands.)

WHITNEY.—and for the next few months I'd like you to keep a journal—writing down things you connect to Nam. Watch TV. What are your responses—direct—indirect—to what you see? Bring the journals in and we'll read to each other, okay? Guess that's it for this evening.

(WOMEN shift places to denote week's passage. SISSY sits upstage center bench.)

WHITNEY. All right—now for tonight—Sissy? You bring in something to read?

SISSY. *(Nods. To audience.)* "I watch MASH. Since I came back I've watched MASH. Current. Reruns. Everything. I cry. Every time. Doesn't matter what the story is. Face of a grunt I cry. Chopper in the sky I cry. Color khaki on the screen I cry. Sad ... terribly sad to

me—all of it ..." (*SHE looks around, starting to tear up.*)
I'm sad *now*—just all so sad—

WHITNEY. *What's* so sad, Sissy?

SISSY. (*Shrugging.*) I don't know—just sad—

WHITNEY. (*Gently.*) What?

SISSY. I don't know—why he said that—

WHITNEY. Who?

SISSY. The picture ...

WHITNEY. On the screen? MASH?

SISSY. (*Looks at Whitney.*) He gave it to me—the
picture—"Remember me"—right in my arms—a soldier—
Christmas—

(*SHE can't go on. MARYJO turns out from group towards
audience.*)

MARYJO. (*Really to herself.*) God I hated Christmas—
dancing in the wards.

SISSY. (*To Whitney.*)We were very close!

MARYJO. (*Still to herself, turned front.*) Telling dying
men how great they looked—

WHITNEY. The boy? At Christmas time?

SISSY. Bill! We were going to get engaged! And Rory
goes, "Shut the shit up! Take a drink and let's get out of
here and shut the shit up!" My fault—my fault—I want to
kill myself sometimes—you know that? Lots of times—

WHITNEY. No! None of it's your fault! None of it!
You hear me Sissy? But you can be sad if you want.
Mourn if you want. That's no crime Sissy. Don't have to
"shut the shit up" anymore!

(THEY all shift. STEELE now sits upstage center bench.)

WHITNEY. Steeley?

STEELE. Well, you know on Sunday mornings I fix me a leisurely breakfast, sit down, and watch Charles Kuralt on TV—because he is not dire news! But this Sunday they are talking about Beirut and I can't sit still! Can't read! Can't eat! Start writing instead: "Same thing is happening! Just like Nam. Sending our good men over there. Setting up another no-win situation. And in the end what is the point of our messing around there anyhow? And what is the point of officials only telling us what they want us to know? And not letting the new come at us straight? What is the point of the brass refusing to look at THE TRUTH?"

WHITNEY. You want them to, Steeley?

STEELE. Spent my whole time disseminating truth! Know where it got me? IGNORED! Know where it got the boys I tried to save? KILLED!

MARTHA. The brass ignored us all. Didn't even keep track of how many women served—no official list.

STEELE. Kept track of how many enemy weapons we captured though, didn't they? And how many innocent civilians we massacred? The brass surely kept track of that!

MARYJO. *(Suddenly jumps up.)* We got raped—

STEELE. What?

SISSY. Oh God—

MARYJO. Fucking brass—

STEELE. The brass?

MARYJO. One room shack ... near Nha Trang ... they ... they didn't come back on the truck for us ... gig was through ... we just found the shack ... no food ... no water

... VC all over the place and not even any money between us to bribe them with so they could help us get out of there—then uh—uh—we're there two days—and uh—uh—the door bursts open—and these six grunts off the field come in—and we're happy—so happy to see them—we think we're safe—(*Pause.*) They didn't give a damn—neither of them—

WHITNEY. Who?

MARYJO. The brass! Headquarters! Saigon! We reported it there afterwards. We needed medical attention—we needed help—we—they smirked! The two colonels *smirked*! Laughing sideways at each other out of their mouths! It was worse than what happened with the grunts. Like it was our fault!

STEELE. (*Takes hold of her.*) Come on—I'll drive you home—

LEEANN. (*Immediately rises, starts talking, moves out of the square. Her anger and rage mount as she speaks*) "I see the hostages from Iran on TV. And this is pissing me off! *They* are getting into limos for this big parade with this *Yellow Ribbon Welcome* and what did *they* do? Sat around four hundred days reading comic books while *I* was risking my life? Getting cursed and spit at in my uniform? And I never even fucking volunteered for that stinking hole in the first place! I wanted Hawaii—where everybody looked LIKE ME?!? Well they sure LOOKED LIKE ME!" (*Starts kicking empty bench which SHE kicks over, stomping on it.*) I start kicking the TV set in my living room. I can't help it! I can't stop! I want to break it to pieces! Break everything to pieces! Break and tear and

strangle that GOOK TO PIECES! PIECES!! ME TO
PIECES!! *ME*!!

MARTHA. (*Grabs her, tries holding her down.*) Here—
here—

LEEANN. (*Trying to wrench free.*) No! Don't you
touch me! You don't know what this is like for me!! None
of you know—I could kill someone—you know that? I
could kill—*me*—(*SHE is in Martha's arms, MARTHA
supporting her.*) Me—me—me—

WHITNEY. (*Catching Martha off guard.*) Martha?

MARTHA. I don't know.

WHITNEY. (*Pursues her.*) Well, you connect to
something on TV?

MARTHA. G.I. in a movie—looks like the guy in my
dream—(*MARTHA turns away.*)

WHITNEY. (*Pursuing.*) What'd he look like?

MARTHA. Me—

WHITNEY. Looks like you?

MARTHA. Thinks like me.

WHITNEY. How?

MARTHA. Serves his country in a war—like he
should—

WHITNEY. How's that?

MARTHA. Dies! Coffin coming off that plane at
Oakland—floating off in The River of Blood—(*MARTHA
turns away.*)

WHITNEY. (*Still pursing.*) You saw that on TV?

MARTHA. Yes! No! (*MARTHA faces Whitney.*) I
don't know—

WHITNEY. You want to read?

MARTHA. (*MARTHA decides, moves to downstage
center bench. Gives it a push. Sits, filled with anger.*

Looks out at audience.) "You people! Whoever you are! Who sent me over there, made me do all those terrible things: waste lives, time, money, resources, *me*! You are not accountable and you will never be accountable. You are hiding behind so many other people you will never be brought to justice in this world! You will never be reckoned with in this world! I WANT YOUR DAY OF RECKONING TO BE AT HAND! I WANT YOU TO BURN FOREVER IN THE HELL OF VIETNAM!" I WANT! I WANT! I WANT!

(By now MARTHA is up looking at others in group. STEELE has moved to side, slowly STEELE begins to sing, back three-quarter to audience.
SHE sings first line of anti-war spiritual.)

WHITNEY. *(To group.)* I want to never to fight another war.
SISSY. *(To group.)* Never again.

(STEELE sings last line of the anti-war spiritual.)

LEEANN. *(To group.)* I want to never be controlled by war.
MARYJO. *(To group.)* Never again.

(STEELE repeats last line of the anti-war spiritual.)

MARTHA. *(To group.)* I want to control war.

(STEELE repeats last line of the anti-war spiritual.

A beat. SHE turns to audience.)

STEELE. I retired *CW3* after thirty years. Settled in D.C. to be near old Walter Wonderful Reed Hospital. 'Cause I've still got trouble with the back. Workin' on my Ph.D. Topic of Dissertation: "Life Management Systems of Persons with Hidden Periodically Manifested and Non-observable Physical Disabilities"! Just about tells it like it is, doesn't it though? (*SHE chuckles.*) Keeps me busy—off the streets. Helps me not give myself a chance to fall over Nam! I already took *that* fall! (*SHE chuckles again.*)

(SISSY comes forward, moving into position, where SHE stood at start of play, putting her coat back on.)

SISSY. (*To audience.*) I became a Born Again Christian. Something opened up in me—I start talking— about life and death and God—I feel Jesus very close! I feel he will help me with Danielle. I feel he's on my side! I go back to school for a Master's in Pastoral Psych. I set up my own practice—*my* way! Counselling my patients to feel harmony—and God! I will *not* prolong that war! I will *not* prolong the chaos in my patients! I try to bring them peace. I love them. Thank you Jesus for them. And I have a little son—six months old and healthy! Thank you Jesus for him! And I have Danielle whom I love and a husband I love and friends I love and my red gambrel house in Massachusetts that I love! Thank you Jesus! For all of that!

(MARTHA comes forward to position at start of play putting on coat.)

MARTHA. (*To audience*.) I'm a counsellor. Vet Centers. Rap groups for women vets. I lecture cross-country to vets' groups. "There are women vets in the military, with needs. They are in combat, and they die in combat even though they *never* carry a gun!" I rejoin the Reserves and teach again. I tell student nurses: "It will *not* be your glorious childhood dream of Florence Nightingale come true! It will be hell on earth! You will *never* get over it afterwards! So get ready! Get set!" I go on TV. I give interviews. I am out there! Personally responsible! They may terminate me very soon. (*SHE laughs*.) "Tightrope walker," that's me! *In* the Establishment preaching *anti-*Establishment! Not politically correct to be honest. But honest—which is *never* politically correct!

LEEANN. (*Puts on coat. To audience*.) I'm a lobbyist with a lot of causes. POW's and MIA's. Amerasian children left in Vietnam. Victims of Agent Orange. I push the Agent Orange Bill through my state. To get money for research and counselling. I write letters, see Representatives, get vets to testify. *Then* the Governor signs the bill—it's passed! And then the Governor calls *me up*! "There's a national salute date for Vietnam Vets in Washington and do you want to be State Coordinator of the event?" "You *bet* I do!"

STEELE. (*Moves a step or two to new area, putting on coat. To audience*.) The five days in Washington when they dedicate The Wall are beautiful—a homecoming—a gathering together—a reunion.

SISSY. (*Steps into new area. To audience.*) We're wearing our boonie hats telling where we were in Nam—what outfit—what place—

MARTHA. (*Joins them. To audience.*) Sometimes we paste our names on our backs—

LEEANN. (*Joins them. To audience.*) And then we walk around the streets of Washington—the whole five days—and through the hotel lobbies—

SISSY. Looking—looking—

STEELE. (*To audience.*) We post notices on the bulletin boards in the hotels—"Jimmy Klein. Private First Class. Company C. 5th Battalion; 60th Infantry; 9th Infantry Division, 1968! Looking for Rusty, Luck & Champ."

SISSY. (*To audience.*) Everyone looking—looking—

STEELE. (*To audience.*) "Reunion Party. 2nd Battalion; 1st Marine Regiment; First Marine Division; We Start at 9 p.m., So Come On!"

LEEANN. Hoping to find someone you served with.

SISSY. A G.I. you nursed back to health—

MARTHA. Sometimes I didn't know which lists of names to look at—the names on the bulletin boards in the hotels—or the names on The Wall—

(*Patriotic MUSIC begins in background. STEELE, SISSY, LEEANN, MARTHA all sit on downstage center bench together.*)

STEELE. (*To audience.*) There was a wonderful ceremony at The Wall. And all of us went. And there were vets just all over the place there—

SISSY. (*To audience.*) In jeans and fatigues and beards—

MARTHA. (*To audience.*) With sleeping bags and camping gear—sleeping in front of The Wall—living on C rations there—blowing the trumpet for reveille—

(To each other.)

SISSY. How *great* to just be here!

MARTHA. Cheering—

LEEANN. Yelling—

SISSY. Screaming—

MARTHA. (*To others.*) Oh God I'm proud!

STEELE. Three thousand vets here today—

LEEANN. Looking—looking—three thousand vets strong—

STEELE. Happy—

MARTHA. Laughing—

STEELE. And getting very dirty looks from those World War II vets! Who are being very solemn around here today!

(THEY laugh.)

LEEANN. Oh God! Maybe—maybe good stuff will start to happen for us now.

SISSY. Maybe we'll find someone—

MARTHA. (*To audience.*) And then—they gave us a 21-gun salute!

(THEY rise, as:)

MALE. (*Voice over.*) COMMENCE FIRE!

(*Blast of ARTILLERY heard, seen firing in sky.*)

MALE. (*Voice over.*) COMMENCE FIRE!

(*Blast of another ROUND heard and seen.*)

MALE. (*Voice over.*) COMMENCE FIRE!

(*BLAST heard and seen again. Huge round of APPLAUSE, CHEERING, WHISTLING. MUSIC stops.*)

MASTER OF CEREMONIES. (*Voice over.*) Thank you. Thank you ... thank you! We are gathered here today to honor the brave men and women who served so well—and gave so much. (*APPLAUSE, CHEERING. His speech continues under.*)
    SISSY. Ceremony's starting—come on—
    LEEANN. Let's get closer.

(*SISSY, LEEANN, STEELE, MARTHA move to background on platforms. Now names on wall become visible. We are at The Wall. MARYJO comes forward. SHE is in her coat.*)

MARYJO. I come to The Wall alone tonight and stop, frozen, staring.
    WHITNEY. (*Steps forward.*) Wanting to connect.
    MARYJO. To all the vets touching the Wall.
    WHITNEY. And the Gold Star mothers.

MARYJO. And the fathers.

WHITNEY. And the children and wives.

MARYJO. And the fifty-eight thousand names that are shining back—

WHITNEY. And then I start to touch the names.

MARYJO. And I can touch them all! And I can feel myself joining with everyone and everything that's here.

WHITNEY. I love this wall!

MARYJO. (*To audience.*) I have come here to leave my guitar—for my beautiful guys! That I sang my heart out to—long ago— (*SHE takes guitar from case.*)

WHITNEY. I light a candle. For my guys I wrote Christmas cards for as they lay dying on the Wards long ago. (*SHE kneels. Puts candle on ground. Lights it. It sends up reflected light.*)

STEELE. (*Now steps near Wall. To audience.*) I come here—take out that old report—(*SHE pulls report out of pocket.*) Yellow—raggedy—"50,000 Chinese"—(*SHE lays report at The Wall.*) I figure it's where this report belongs—

SISSY. (*Looking at Wall.*) I find the name of the soldier who took my picture. Bob Hope Show. (*SHE takes out photo.*) I'm giving the picture back to you. (*SHE puts the picture down at Wall.*) Forever—soldier boy—

MARTHA. (*Steps close, looking at Wall.*) My nurse's cap. For all the brave and dying boys I cared for. When I was Head Nurse. On Duty. Vietnam! (*SHE puts cap at Wall, then gives a smart military salute to The Wall.*)

(*LEEANN comes into area, on high platform looking at Wall, then turns toward audience.*)

LEEANN. (*To audience.*) Midnight. The candle making a haloed light on all the names. I have only one name I know to find, and I've come to leave him my diary, but it is too dark to see. So I walk along The Wall—looking—wanting to thank that soldier for his hooch and his psychedelic lights and his goddamn Led Zeppelin music that kept me from going crazy in Vietnam—(*SHE leaves her diary.*)

MARYJO. And then for the first time in almost twenty years—I start to play. (*She begins strumming, AMERICA THE BEAUTIFUL, then singing, very softly.*) OH BEAUTIFUL FOR SPACIOUS SKIES, FOR AMBER WAVES OF GRAIN (*Music on guitar continues softly under until end of play.*)

LEEANN. And then—I see a Vet—on a cane—

(*A VET enters, walking slowly, boonie hat, fatigues, on a cane, limping along The Wall climbing to a high platform. Slowly—slowly he comes along The Wall—OTHERS turn to watch scene. In the back ground MARYJO's MUSIC is heard, softly.*)

VET. (*Coming to Leeann.*) Hey—you a nurse?

LEEANN. Yes.

VET. Where were you in Nam?

LEEANN. 11th Evac.

VET. When?

LEEANN. '69 to '70—

VET. I got hit in '70—

LEEANN. Oh?

VET. I thought I knew you! I know you!

LEEANN. I don't think so soldier—there were so many—and it's so dark here—I don't—

VET. I'd know you anywhere! You took care of me!

LEEANN. Yes? Well—maybe—always a chance—maybe I did—

VET. (*Puts down his cane.*) Hey—nurse? Watch this! (*HE now takes a step or two toward her.*)

LEEANN. You a double amp?

VET. Yes, ma'am, I am!

LEEANN. Oh soldier, you are beautiful!

(Around Vet's neck HE wears a lei of yellow ribbons. HE now takes this and puts it around her neck.)

VET. Here, ma'am—this is for you! Welcome home!

(And HE takes her in his arms and THEY kiss, then embrace deeply.)

MARYJO. *(Still plaintive, melancholy, now sings out:)* AMERICA, AMERICA GOD SHED HIS GRACE ON THEE, AND CROWN THY GOOD WITH BROTHERHOOD, FROM SEA TO SHINING SEA.

(MARYJO now steps to The Wall and quietly lays her guitar against it. All three turn to look out at audience. OTHERS now turn to look at audience. LIGHTS to BLACK.)

END OF PLAY

COSTUME PLOT

<u>AMERICAN MAN</u>
ACT I
O.D. T-Shirt
O.D. Jacket
O.D. Pants
Black Combat Boots
Dog Tags
O.D. Baseball Caps
O.D. Shirt
O.D. Boonie Hat
Camo Jacket
ACT II
Khaki Shirt
Khaki Pants
Black Tearaway Tie
Blue 12 OD Jacket
Black Shoes
Blue Sweater Vest
Blue Blazer
Khaki Billfold Cap
O.D. Pants
Camo Jacket
O.D. Flak Jacket
Camo Boonie Hat
Black Combat Boots
<u>WHITNEY</u>
ACT I
Plaid Kilt Skirt
Pale Yellow Oxford Shirt
Camel Wrap Coat w/Fur Collar w/self belt

Brown Suede Loafers
Khaki Apron w/White Cross on bib
Camo Shirt
Flesh Hose
Yellow Headband
ACT II
Maroon Tweed Pants
Turquoise Silk Blouse
Maroon Wedge Shoes
O.D. Shirt
Camel Wrap Coat w/Fur Collar w/self belt
MARY JO
ACT I
White Leather Mini Skirt w/Brown Suede Leather Western
   Trim
White Leather Vest w/Fringe and Western Trims
Pale Orange Stretch Top
White Cowboy Boots
White Cowboy Hat
Red Vinyl Mini Raincoat w/Belt
Camo Rain Cape
Suntan Hose
ACT II
Camo Rain Cape
Maroon Velvet Stretch Top
Maroon/Blue Floral Print Velvet Mini Skirt
Black Heels w/Strap
Black Hose
Red Vinyl Raincoat

STEELE
ACT I
Class A Summer Uniform w/Cap
Khaki Rain Cape
Neutral Silk Scarf
Black Oxfords
Black Beret
Flesh Hose
Gold Tank Leotard
Camo Jacket
Dogtags
ACT II
Khaki Pants
Beige Silk Kimono-Style Jacket
Silk Jacket
Black Suede Shoes
Khaki Rain Cape
Gold Tank Leotard
Black Knee Highs
Neutral Silk Scarf
Camo Jacket
Class A Cap
Dogtags
MARTHA
ACT I
Beige Jeans
Pale Blue and White Tearaway Middy
O.D. Tank
Brown Oxfords
O.D. Shirt
Navy Blue Leather Wrap Coat w/self belt
Beige Socks

Dogtags
ACT II
Black Jeans
Maroon/Blue Print Silk Blouse
Rust/Brown Checked Jacket w/Tie
Black Socks
Black Suede Oxfords
Navy Blue Wrap Leather Coat
Dogtags
<u>LEEANN</u>
ACT I
Bell-Bottom Blue Jeans
Gray/Lavender T-Shirt
Faded Denim Vest
Yellow Bandanna [Bien]
Leather Head Band
O.D. Shirt
Beige Suede Shoes
Iridescent Silk A-line Raincoat
ACT II
Light Grey/Green Asian Fabric Blouse
Dark Rose Asian-Style cut and trim Vest
Black Silk Pants
Black Flats
Camo Shirt
Iridescent Silk A-line Raincoat
<u>SISSY</u>
ACT I
White Turtle Neck
Pink Tearaway Jumper
White Tights

Otter Mary-Jane Shoes
O. D. Jumpsuit
Dark Turquoise Princess Coat
Gold Cross on Chain
ACT II
Brown/Rust Country Print Long-sleeved Dress
Brown Leather Boots
Camo Shirt
Dark Turquoise Princess Coat

PROPERTY PLOT

4 BAMBOO BENCHES: 5'x1'6"
SANDBAGS
4 GREEN FLIGHT BAGS
1 GRAY FLIGHT BAG
SUITCASE: APPROX. 16"x20"x6"
GUITAR (MARTIN NEW YORKER)
2 PR. CLAVE STICKS
DUFFLE BAG HAND MICROPHONE (ON
  CORD: PRACTICAL)
GREEN WINE BOTTLE: NO LABEL
4 ROCKS GLASSES
YELLOW RIBBON
JOINTS (3)
SMALL DIARY WITH PENCIL
ASHTRAY WITH LID
BREAKAWAY WHISKEY BOTTLE (BROWN)
1 STRAND X-MAS TREE LIGHTS (OUTDOOR
  BULBS)
VOTIVE CANDLE #1 (WITH RED GLASS HOLDER)
BOXED MATCHES
KODAK 126x CAMERA WITH FLASHCUBE
PICTURE OF SISSY
REPORT: HARD FOLDER WITH POCKETS
INCL: NEWSPAPER CLIPPINGS, SMALL YELLOW
  LOOSE SHEETS PAPER, MAPS, FILE FOLDER
  WITH HAND WRITTEN REPORT ON YELLOW
  PAPER.
6 STRONG BEAM, GREEN FLASHLIGHTS
.45 ARMY PISTOL

6 C-RATION CANS W/SAND (ASHTRAYS)
8 BOOKS OF MATCHES
WHISKEY FLASK (CLEAR, NO LABEL)
MARLBORO CIGARETTES
GUITAR CASE (MARTIN NEW YORKER)
ZIPPO LIGHTER
3 BROWN BEER BOTTLES: NO LABELS
GOLD CIGARETTE CASE
GOLD LIGHTER
CLEAR WHISKEY BOTTLE: NO LABEL
BIC LIGHTER
MERIT ULTRA LIGHT CIGARETTES
VOTIVE CANDLE #2
AGED PICTURE OF SISSY
AGED REPORT: FILE FOLDER W/YELLOW PAGES
NAVY NURSE CAP
AGED YELLOW RIBBON
WOODEN CANE
LEI: YELLOW RIBBONS & FLOWERS
NEWPORT LIGHT CIGARETTES
PENCIL

PERSONAL PROPS

G.I.:	Sissy picture #1, Yellow Ribbon #1
WHITNEY:	Gray flight bag
SISSY:	Green flight bag, Cross on chain
STEELE:	Green flight bag
LEEANN:	Green flight bag
MARTHA:	Green flight bag
MARYJO:	Suitcase, Guitar

Duffel Bag Presets

STEELE
Act I
Report folder in pocket
Camo jacket/w gun
Purse w/hat, cig. case w/ 4 Newports, ashtray w/lid,
pencil, matches
Flashlight & scarf
Act II
Robe & scarf
Hat, cigarette case
Earrings, Beret
Overcoat w/report #2
SISSY
Act I
Camo jacket
Belt in pocket
Flight suit
Act II
Coat w/ picture #2
MARTHA
Act I
Navy nurse cap in pocket
Camo jacket
Green OD shirt
Marlboros, 2 joints, matches
Act II
Navy nurse cap in pocket
Coat
Blazer

MARYJO
Act I
Fringed vest
Act II
Rain coat
LEEANN
Act I
Camo boonie hat in pocket
Green OD shirt w/diary & pencil in right pocket
Act II
Boonie hat
Coat w/diary & ribbon
WHITNEY
Act I
Red cross apron in pocket
Camo jacket
Act II
Coat w/candle, matches, hair clip

Prop Placement

BACKSTAGE
UR Zippo lighter
Marlboro cigarettes
UL
Guitar case
Lei
Cane
Ashtray
ONSTAGE
Above Platform B, in clips: 4 flashlights
In sandbag SR of Platform B: 1 set claves, camera with
  flash, canteen of water

<u>In sandbag SR of Platform D:</u> cowboy hat, camo poncho, flask with 1 inch of tea, 1 flashlight, C-can with matches & 1 Newport, glass with water, Microphone w/cord

<u>In sandbag SL of Platform D:</u> 2 empty rocks glasses, wine bottle filled with water, candle & boxed matches, breakaway bottle, C-can w/matches & 1 Newport cig., canteen of water

<u>SL of Platform C, on hook:</u> X-mas tree lights

<u>DR of Platform B:</u> C-can w/1 Newport cig.

<u>Other C-cans w/matches:</u> under stair units 1 & 2, SL of stair unit 2

NAMES ON WALL

In the Manhattan Theatre Club production, light boxes were mounted behind specially-constructed corrugated fiberglass panels to create the Vietnam Memorial. These fiberglass panels served as the facing to each platform and stair. The panels consisted of a layer of scrim painted to match the overall set color, then adhered directly onto the outside of clear corrugated fiberglass, which actually looks slightly frosted. Then a light-weight muslin layer bearing the names of those killed in action was adhered onto the backside of the "clear" fiberglass panel. This muslin layer was prepared in advance and bore the names of those killed in action. The names were applied to the muslin layer by laying them out in three-inch helvetica press-on letters. Then four coats of flat black latex paint were sprayed on top of the press-on letters to opaque the area around them. After the muslin was opaque, it was sprayed with one last coat of paint that matched on the front of the scrim. The letters were then removed, creating a reverse screen of clear letters on an opaqued background. As described above, the muslin was then glued directly onto the back of the fiberglass panels.

These panels were then mounted directly onto the light boxes, which were approximately twelve inches deep and contained about 2400 watts. The MTC production used four light boxes. The light boxes, now bearing their fiberglass panels, were then mounted beneath each platform and stair.

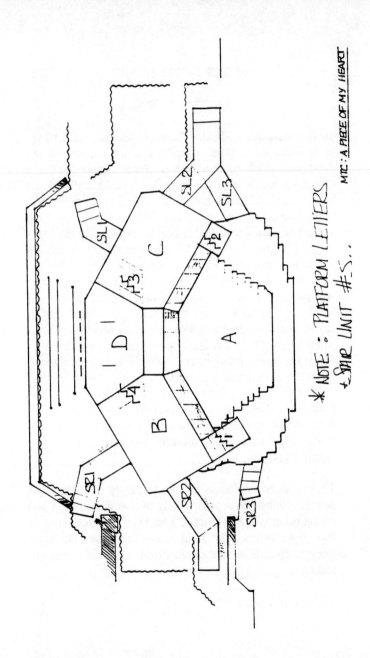

* NOTE : PLATFORM LETTERS
+ SPLR UNIT #5...

MTC : _A PIECE OF MY HEART_